Martin Nicholas Kunz

best designed

hotel pools

INDOOR & OUTDOOR . CONTEMPORARY MINIMALISTIC . ROOFTOP . NATURAL CURVES

avedition

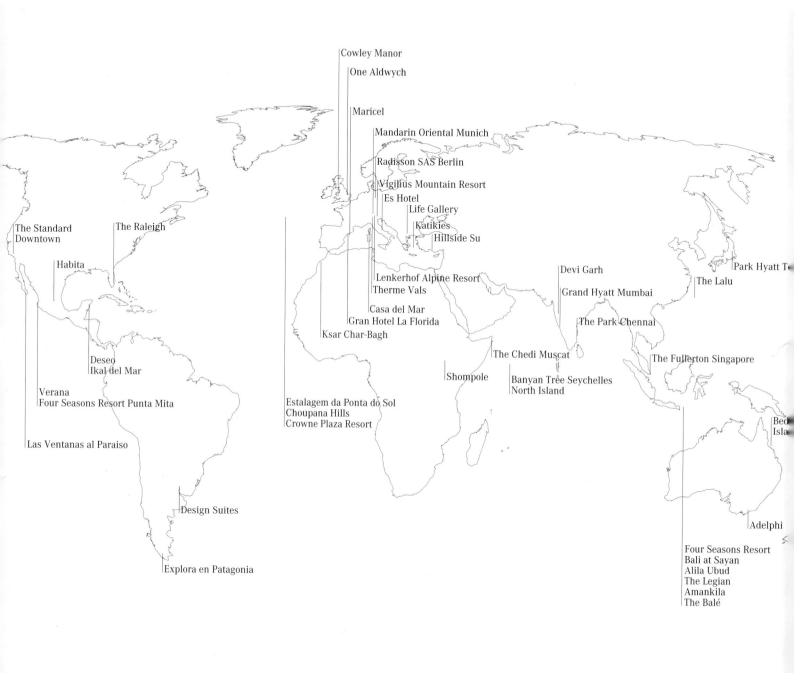

The Standard
Downtown

The Raleigh

Cowley Manor

One Aldwych

Maricel

Mandarin Oriental Munich

Radisson SAS Berlin

Vigilius Mountain Resort

Es Hotel

Life Gallery

Katikies

Hillside Su

Park Hyatt T

The Lalu

Habita

Devi Garh

Grand Hyatt Mumbai

Lenkerhof Alpine Resort
Therme Vals

The Park Chennai

Casa del Mar
Gran Hotel La Florida

Ksar Char-Bagh

The Fullerton Singapore

Deseo
Ikal del Mar

The Chedi Muscat

Verana
Four Seasons Resort Punta Mita

Shompole

Banyan Tree Seychelles
North Island

Estalagem da Ponta do Sol
Choupana Hills
Crowne Plaza Resort

Las Ventanas al Paraiso

Bed
Isla

Design Suites

Adelphi

Explora en Patagonia

Four Seasons Resort
Bali at Sayan
Alila Ubud
The Legian
Amankila
The Balé

The Chedi Muscat, Jean-Michel Gathy, Yasuhiro Koichi.   Grand Hyatt Mumbai, Bilkey Linas Design, Lohan Associates

As human beings existing in a solid space, one experiences floors, ceilings, walls, corners and every detail that forms this differently than in a fluid space. Every existing setting is seen in a different perspective, where the body firmly stands as the air blows our skin. Moreover, time records itself on the solid surface, encapsulating every second in the air bouncing against the walls. Stepping into a fluid space brings one's inner feelings into reconciliation with this natural element, water, purifying our soul and padding our skin with every molecule. This book illustrates this element with the best-designed hotel pools divided into different categories: indoor, indoor &

outdoor, contemporary minimalistic, rooftop, and curve and natural form pools. In this compilation, you will find a fluid variety that could fit your mood: choose a setting and float in time.

An indoor pool defines its borders between interior and exterior, compensating itself with the use of materials and light. Similar to this, the indoor & outdoor pools bring in a natural flow into the interior by connecting both water surfaces into one, breaking the barrier and allowing a continuous flow from one to the other. A different focus is applied in contemporary minimalistic pools, concentrating more in a

minimum expression, integrating individuals into a contemporary mood. In rooftop pools the flow changes dramatically up high, reaching out for the energy flowing in the urban setting, to become an intimate public space. Finally, curves and natural form pools are a natural creation that clearly adapt to their context to continue in harmony, respecting the natural curves and layers of the earth to form a space that complements with the human natural creation. This solid book and fluid experiences are to be merged into ONE ultimate experience, liquefying time and space through the sounds and waves that will always prevail with us throughout time.

Bedarra Island, Engelen Moore.   Life Gallery, Klein & Heller, Vasilis Rodatos.

Fester Grund ist statisch. Ganz anders im Wasser. Jede Bewegung erzeugt eine neue Form, eröffnet eine neue Perspektive. Wer seinen Körper ganz bewusst in die „Leichtigkeit" von Wasser eintaucht, spürt den stetigen Wandel der Flüssigkeit und die Kraft der Reinigung. Das vorliegende Buch widmet sich dem Element Wasser von einer seiner schönsten Seiten. „best designed hotel pools" fasst ästhetische Schwimmbadarchitektur rund um den Globus zusammen und zeigt, wie Wasser ideenreich „eingefangen" werden kann. Die hier gezeigten Beispiele in den insgesamt 45 Hotels sind aber nicht nur eine sprudelnde Inspirationsquelle.

Wer die nötige Zeit und bei einigen Beispielen auch das nötige Kleingeld aufbringt, kann selbst seine Badesachen einpacken und an den „Originalschauplätzen" ins Wasser springen. Sei dies in eines der Hallenbäder aus der Rubrik „Indoor Pools", aus „Indoor Outdoor Pools", „Contemporary Minimalistic" oder „Natural Curves". Wer beim Schwimmen in einem Stadthotel den Ausblick nicht vermissen möchte oder gar den Nervenkitzel in schwindelerregenden Höhen sucht, dem sei ein Testbad in einem der „Rooftop Pools" empfohlen. Die ausgewählten Hallenbäder bestechen durch ihre Materialauswahl sowie

durch den Umgang mit Licht. Die Rubrik „Indoor Outdoor Pools" zeigt Lösungen, die sich mit fließenden Übergängen zwischen gestalteten Innenräumen und gewachsenen Formen der Natur beschäftigen. Die Beispiele in „Contemporary Minimalistic" zeigen, wie man durch die geschickte Kombination von Materialien, Farben und mit dekorativen Details Stimmungen erzielen kann. Ideenreichtum bei wenig Platz ist das Thema der Schwimmbäder auf den Hoteldächern der Welt. Das abschließende Kapitel widmet sich den in natürlichen Formen gebauten Schwimmbädern und vervollständigt die erfrischende Architekt-Tour um den Globus.

indoor pools

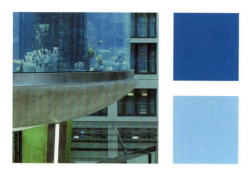

radisson sas | berlin .germany
DESIGN: BHPS Architekten

Water is the dominant element in Radisson SAS. The hotel boasts of rooms with an ocean view – although to be perfectly frank it is located far from the ocean right in the middle of the German capital across from the Berlin Dome. Indeed offering a view of the water, the hotel surrounds a large atrium, in the middle of which stands the "Aquedon", a huge glass cylinder housing the largest round aquarium in the world. One million liters of saltwater is home to 2,500 tropical fish. More than 100 of the 427 hotel rooms have an unobstructed view of this sparkling underwater world. The wet element also plays a central role in the hotel's wellness area. After a steam bath or a visit to the organic or Finnish sauna, guests can refresh themselves under the torrents of a waterfall shower. A counter-current pool offers a great swim workout. Because the Radisson is centrally located, the pool is situated within the building. Large reddish-brown natural-stone facing covers the walls, exuding an extravagant flair, while luminous rings on top of the pillars ease the pull of gravity and compensate for the lack of daylight.

Wasser ist das bestimmende Element im Radisson SAS. Das Hotel rühmt sich seiner Zimmer mit Meerblick, und das, obwohl es fernab vom nächsten Ozean liegt, genauer gesagt mitten in der deutschen Hauptstadt, dem Berliner Dom gegenüber. Der Clou ist ein großes Atrium, in dessen Zentrum der „Aquadom" steht, ein riesiger Glaszylinder, der das größte runde Aquarium der Welt aufnimmt: In einer Million Liter Salzwasser schwimmen 2500 tropische Fische. Aus über 100 der 427 Zimmer hat der Gast Aussicht auf diese Unterwasserwelt. Auch im Wellnessbereich des Hotels spielt das feuchte Element die zentrale Rolle. Nach einem Dampfbad, dem Besuch der Bio-Sauna oder der finnischen Sauna kann der Gast sich unter einer Schwall- oder einer Wasserfallbrause erfrischen. Zum sportlichen Schwimmen lädt ein Becken mit Gegenstromanlage ein. Wegen der zentralen Lage des Radisson liegt der Pool im Inneren des Gebäudes. Eine rötlich braune Verkleidung aus großen Natursteinplatten an der Wand verleiht ihm Noblesse, während Leuchtringe am Kopf der Säulen dem Raum die Schwere nehmen und den Mangel an Tageslicht kompensieren sollen.

one aldwych | london . united kingdom
DESIGN: Mary Fox-Linton, Gordon Campbell Gray

To integrate a swimming pool into an existing building is not an easy task. It becomes even more difficult if the building was built almost 100 years ago. Amazing how this venture succeeded in One Aldwych, especially since the original purpose of the building was meant to be not a hotel but home to the newspaper "The Morning Post" in 1907. The 18m pool, besprinkling guests with underwater music, had to be accommodated in the basement. But in contrast to many dreary and overloaded wellness landscapes located in basements, the architecture here contributes a decisive feeling of well-being. Extensive use of glass provides lightness, and yellow walls give an almost sunny atmosphere. Only the old riveted steel beams, still evident in these modern surroundings, reveal the true history of this building.

Ein Schwimmbad nachträglich in ein Gebäude zu integrieren ist nie einfach. Noch schwieriger wird es, wenn der Bau bereits vor knapp hundert Jahren errichtet wurde. Erstaunlich, wie gut dieses Unterfangen im One Aldwych geglückt ist, das zudem nie als Hotel geplant war, sondern 1907 als Sitz der Zeitung „The Morning Post" entstand. Der 18 Meter lange Pool, der den Gast mit Unterwassermusik „berieselt", musste im Untergeschoss Platz finden. Im Unterschied zu vielen anderen oft düsteren oder überladenen Wellnesslandschaften in Kelleretagen ist die Architektur hier ein entscheidender Wohlfühlfaktor. Viel Glas sorgt für Leichtigkeit, gelbe Wandflächen für eine beinahe sonnige Atmosphäre. Nur die alten genieteten Stahlpfeiler erzählen in diesem modernen Ambiente noch von der Geschichte des Gebäudes.

design suites | buenos aires . argentina
DESIGN: Ernesto Goransky

Design-Suites-Hotel presents itself as a modern and puristic complex, situated in the heart of the Argentinean capital. The stylish Ricoleta-Quarter, Santa Fe and Calao Streets, and the Retiro Station are located in the immediate vicinity. It is not only the architecture that is minimalist but also the pool in the literal sense of the word. A small basin only a few feet in length greets the guests. Lack of space is compensated by daylight streaming in through the glass ceiling, a rarity for pools in centrally located hotels. And to pass the time, swimming guests can keep an eye on the happenings in the adjoining bar. In short: not for long-distance swimmers but for spontaneous divers looking for a refreshing dip.

Modern und puristisch präsentiert sich das Design-Suites-Hotel, das im Herzen der argentinischen Hauptstadt liegt. Das schicke Ricoleta-Viertel, die Santa Fe- und die Calao-Street und der Retiro-Bahnhof befinden sich in unmittelbarer Nachbarschaft. Minimalistisch ist nicht nur die Architektur, sondern auch der Pool, und zwar im wahren Sinne des Wortes: Ein schmales Becken von nur wenigen Metern Länge erwartet den Gast. Den Mangel an Platz macht es mit Tages-licht wett, denn es ist glasüberdeckt, was bei Pools von zentral gelegenen Hotels keine Selbstverständlichkeit ist. Zusätzlich kann der Gast vom Becken aus das Treiben in der Bar verfolgen, die sich direkt daneben befindet. Kurz und gut: Nichts für ausdauernde Sport-schwimmer, sondern für spontane Erfrischungstaucher.

explora en patagonia | patagonia . chile

DESIGN: German del Sol

The Explora en Patagonia is situated on the shore of the Lake Pehoé, like an anchored ship. In front of the bizarre mountain scenery of the world famous Torres del Paine, the austere, three-floored wooden structure is nestled into the cliffs over the Salto Chico waterfalls. Those spending time here in one of the world's most impressive wildernesses, seek, above all, intimacy combined with nature. Here, luxury is defined by functionality and a restrained style in both the interior as well as the exterior. The indoor pool of the hotel presents itself accordingly; the pool is accommodated in its own bathhouse, the Casa de Baños de Ona. A simple wooden boardwalk leads to it from the hotel. The interior pulls one's gaze from this perspective to the outside and averts from no single detail of the background of the mountains. The over-dimensioned glass front is turned towards the bizarre Torres de Paine. Inside, one finds clarity in form with two periodical window units on the sidewall tracing the panorama on the horizon and dark slate floors framing the elongated pool. The bath-house walls and ceiling are covered with untreated wood lending the room warmth; dispersing its strict geometry in alternation from the horizontal to the diagonal flow of the lines.

Das Explora en Patagonia liegt am Ufer des Lago Pehoé wie ein Schiff vor Anker. Vor der bizarren Bergkulisse der weltberühmten Torres del Paine schmiegt sich der nüchterne, dreistöckige Holzbau an die Felsen oberhalb des Salto-Chico-Wasserfalles. Wer hier in einer der beeindruckendsten Wildnisse der Welt seine Zeit verbringt, sucht vor allem die Nähe zur Natur. Hier definiert sich Luxus über Funktionalität und einen zurückhaltenden Stil, innen wie außen. Dementsprechend präsentiert sich auch das Hallenbad des Hotels. Es befindet sich in einem eigenen Badehaus, dem Casa de Baños de Ona. Zu ihm führt ein schlichter hölzerner Plankenweg vom Hotel. Der Innenraum führt den Blick aus jeder Perspektive nach draußen und lenkt durch kein Detail von der Kulisse der Berge ab. Die überdimensionale Glasfront ist den bizarren Torres del Paine zugewandt. Innen findet man Klarheit in der Form. Zwei regelmäßige Fensterreihen an der Längsseite zeichnen das Panorama am Horizont nach. Dunkler Schieferboden rahmt das langgestreckte Becken ein. Wände und Decke des Badehauses sind in naturbelassenem Holz verkleidet, das dem Raum Wärme verleiht und seine strenge Geometrie im Wechsel der Linienführung von der Waagrechten zur Diagonalen auflöst.

park hyatt tokyo | tokyo . japan
D E S I G N : Fredric Thomas, John Morford

Many of us are familiar with this hotel even though some of us have not physically been there. The hotel plays the third leading role in Sofia Coppola's film work, "Lost in Translation". The exceedingly luxurious atmosphere of the Park Hyatt places one in a different story; where the guest rooms, restaurants, bars, and the all-pervasive panoramic view over the Japanese metropolis make the visitors aware of their own distance from the real life in this city at every moment in time. The glassed peak of the Shinjuku Tower opens up more than just another magnificent view of the Japanese metropolis; in the 47th floor of the skyscraper with a 20-meter long indoor pool. Here, one can swim laps through the subtly shining blue of the basin, mixing with the color of the sky, while enjoying this view in Zen-like peace. The strict symmetry of the room, defined by soaring diagonals, has a lofty and religious effect. During the day, this broad, open hall is a temple of light. At night, the city, way down below, blossoms as a bustling and colorfully flashing scenario. In the middle of Shinjuku, Tokyo's largest business and entertainment district, one finds a free, airy atmosphere here, peace and relaxation.

Dieses Hotel ist vielen von uns vertraut, obwohl wir es noch nie besucht haben. In Sofia Coppolas Kino-Erstlingswerk „Lost in Translation" spielt es neben Bill Murray und Scarlett Johannsson die dritte Hauptrolle. Es ist dabei der weltentrückte Kokon für eine ungewöhnliche Begegnung und die spröde Freundschaft zweier Amerikaner in Tokio, die sich in der Stadt völlig fremd und in ihrem Dasein absolut verloren fühlen. Die Handlung hätte kaum in einem passenderen Rahmen stattfinden können. Der allgegenwärtige Panoramablick über die japanische Metropole macht dem Hotelbesucher die eigene Distanz zum wirklichen Leben in dieser Stadt in jedem Augenblick bewusst. Den Cineasten blieb jedoch ein Raum des Hotels vorenthalten: die gläserne Spitze des Shinjuku Towers, in der sich der 20 Meter lange Indoor Pool befindet. Hier, im 47. Stockwerk, zieht man in Zengleicher Ruhe seine Bahnen durch das subtil leuchtende Blau des Bassins, das sich mit der Farbe des Himmels vermischt. Die strikte Symmetrie des Raums, der von aufstrebenden Diagonalen bestimmt ist, wirkt erhaben und beinahe sakral. Am Tag ist diese weite, offene Halle ein Tempel des Lichts. Bei Nacht erblüht die weit unten liegende City als quirliges und bunt blinkendes Szenario. Mitten in Shinjuku, Tokios größtem Geschäfts- und Ausgehviertel, findet man hier eine freie, luftige Atmosphäre, Ruhe und Entspannung.

vigilius mountain resort | lana . italy

DESIGN: Matteo Thun

Starting in the late afternoon, when the last cable railcar has left for the valley town of Lana, the guest is transported to the Vigiljoch alone with the overpowering silence of the mountain region; 1500 meters over the sea level with a magnificent panoramic view over the Etsch Valley to the Dolomites. Matteo Thun also pays tribute here to the crystal-clear water in the mountain lakes and streams through his designed work of art. The straight indoor pool is completely inlaid with silver quartz from nearby Sterzing. The stones lend the water a natural silvery color. Like waterfalls, the three-massage showers platter over the bathers and let the water dance around them in bubbling waves. In contrast to a heart-attack-cold glacial lake, the 14 x 4 meter pool is comfortably tempered and next to the pool there is an open fireplace. The pool area is visually extended without interruption towards the outside to the sun deck. Countryside and bright larch forests are all around. They surround the hotel and even grow out of the building's interior. The border between the interior and exterior becomes fluid. This is mainly noticeable in the whirlpool leading outside through a glass sliding door. Outside the atmosphere is chillier and harder, changing the aesthetics of the space. On top of the babbling of the water, the cowbells ring far off, combining both rhythms.

Ab dem späten Nachmittag, wenn die letzte Seilbahn in den Talort Lana abgefahren ist, findet der Gast sich auf dem Vigiljoch mit der Stille der Bergwelt allein. Auf 1500 Metern hat er zudem einen grandiosen Rundblick über das Tal der Etsch auf die Dolomiten. Es erscheint nur konsequent, dass Matteo Thun dem kristallklaren Wasser der Bergseen und -bäche mit einem hervorragend gestalteten Pool huldigt. Das geradlinige Innenbecken ist vollkommen mit Silberquarz aus dem nahen Sterzing ausgelegt. Der Stein verleiht dem Wasser eine natürlich-silbrige Farbe. Wie Wasserfälle prasseln drei Massageduschen über den Badenden und lassen sprudelnde Wellen um ihn tanzen. Im Unterschied zu einem eiskalten Gletschersee ist der 14 mal 4 Meter lange Pool angenehm temperiert. Wer dennoch fröstelt, kann neben dem Becken am offenen Kamin den besten Platz zwischen Feuer und Wasser wählen. Optisch ohne Unterbrechung ist das Bad nach außen zur Sonnenterrasse verlängert. Hier dominieren die Landschaft und der helle Lärchenwald, der sogar aus dem Inneren des Gebäudes wächst. Die Grenze zwischen innen und außen ist überall fließend. Am deutlichsten merkt man dies wiederum im Whirlpool, der durch eine gläserne Schiebetür ins Freie führt. Draußen wird die Atmosphäre frischer und die Akustik ändert sich: Außer dem Plätschern des Wassers hört man von fern das Läuten von Kuhglocken.

therme vals | vals . switzerland
DESIGN: Peter Zumthor

Even just the arrival imparts something of the secretive aura with which the Therme Vals fascinates. From the Canton capital of Chur, the hot springs can be reached, either by driving over the upper alpine pass or with the Rhätischen Railway or the post office bus. When entering the pool, water and stone indulge with an incomparable clarity. The Swiss architect Peter Zumthor drafted and built the hot springs as a rectangular structure with layered walls made of Valser quartzite stone slabs, excavated only two kilometers distant. Despite the orthodox strictness of the colors (gray in all variations) and form of the building (rectangular and straight), one is touched by water from the ice-bath through a fragrant blossom bath, up to a steam bath in playful variety. The water here appears to be alive; it gurgles and platters through the partially grotto-like hall simultaneously refreshing and warming one up underneath the sky. Light plays a crucial role in this ambience; the incidence of the daylight mirrors in most varied reflections on the water surfaces; floating in luminous rows and soft shadows on the relief-like surface walls, constantly changing.

Schon die Anreise vermittelt etwas von der geheimnisvollen Aura, mit der die Therme Vals fasziniert. Von der Kantonshauptstadt Chur erreicht man die Therme entweder nach einer Autofahrt über den Oberalppass oder mit der Rhätischen Bahn und dem Postbus. Mehr Zauberberg geht eigentlich nicht. Dann betritt man ein Bad, das als eine einmalige Komposition aus Wasser und Stein geschaffen wurde. Der Schweizer Architekt Peter Zumthor entwarf und baute die Therme als einen rechteckigen Baukörper mit Wänden aus geschichteten dünnen Steinplatten, für die er Valser Quarzit verwendete, der in nur zwei Kilometer Entfernung abgebaut wurde. Die orthodoxe Strenge von Farbe (Grau in allen Varianten) und Form (Rechteck und Quadrat) des Gebäudes steht im Kontrast zu der abwechslungsreichen Vielfalt, in der sich das Element Wasser darbietet: vom Eisbad über ein aromatisches Blütenbad bis hin zum Dampfbad. Das Wasser scheint hier ein lebendes Wesen, es gluckst und plätschert durch die zum Teil grottenähnlichen Hallen oder erfrischt und wärmt zugleich unter freiem Himmel. Das fein nuancierte Spiel von Hell und Dunkel trägt ebenfalls entscheidend zur Atmosphäre bei. Ständig ändert sich der Einfall des Tageslichts, das sich in vielfältigsten Reflexionen auf den Wasserflächen widerspiegelt oder in sanften Schattierungen über die reliefartige Oberfläche der Wände wandert.

indoor outdoor pools

lenkerhof alpine resort | lenk . switzerland

DESIGN: Rolf Balmer

The wellness rooms and the outdoor pool face the park in the interior of the building of the new Lenkerhof Alpine Resort. Wellness areas in the traditional hotels were usually designed in stone and earthy hues; in contrast to this, strong red and blue shades are used here to represent the elements of fire and water, setting the tone in the spa. These elements, facing the blue of the daylight flooding into the adjoining pool area are then mirrored in the entire water surface. Optically, the indoor and outdoor pools are hardly separated from each other. The rectangular basic forms of both pools interlock with each other with a thin dividing line drawn through the glass front, interrupted only by a few simple supports. While the sunlight pleasantly tempers the interior and provides warmth and relaxation, the adjoining outdoor pool imparts the unfiltered power of nature. The Lenker spring's slightly sulphuruous healing waters patter from the massage showers over the body and skin. One can experience the tension between the comfortably tempered spring water, the clear, sometimes cuttingly cold atmosphere, and the powerful sun in the Swiss mountains at 2000 meters above sea level.

Dem Park im Inneren des Gebäude-Ensembles zugewandt, liegen die Wellnessräume und der Außenpool des neuen Lenkerhof Alpine Resort. Während der Wellnessbereich der traditionellen Hotels meist in Stein und erdigen Farben gestaltet ist, kamen hier kräftige Rot- und Blautöne zum Einsatz, die für die Elemente Feuer und Wasser stehen, die das Kurangebot im Spa ausmachen. Dem steht das klare Blau des Tageslichts gegenüber, das den angrenzenden Poolbereich durchflutet und sich in der gesamten Wasserfläche spiegelt. Innen- und Außenbecken sind optisch so gut wie nicht voneinander getrennt; die rechteckigen Grundformen der beiden Pools greifen ineinander. Eine Glasfront, die nur von einigen schmucklosen Stützen unterbrochen wird, zieht lediglich eine dünne Trennlinie. Während das Sonnenlicht den Innenraum angenehm temperiert und für Wärme und Entspannung sorgt, vermittelt der angrenzende Außenpool die ungefilterten Kräfte der Natur. Aus den Massageduschen prasselt das leicht schwefelige Heilwasser der Lenker-Quellen über Haut und Körper. Intensiv fühlt man hier die Spannung zwischen dem wohl temperierten Quellwasser, der klaren, manchmal schneidend kalten Luft und der kraftvollen Sonne in den Schweizer Bergen auf 2000 Meter Meereshöhe.

choupana hills resort & spa | madeira . portugal

DESIGN: Michel de Camaret, Didier Lefort

On a rise near Funchal lies a 20-acre estate with 34 guest villas. Due to its location above a botanical garden, an indulging view includes lush green vegetation as well as the Atlantic Ocean. To enjoy this panorama to the utmost, the planners extensively glassed in the indoor swimming pool. While guests swim in warm water against the flow of the counter-current pool to increase the time it takes to complete the 13.5m lap, they can look through the panorama windows and ponder whether or not to jump in the larger outdoor 250m² pool. The patio surface, consisting of natural stone slab and small planting areas bordered by rubble masonry directly on the pool edge, creates the impression of swimming directly in nature.

Auf einer Anhöhe bei Funchal liegt ein acht Hektar großes Gut mit 34 Gästevillen. Durch die Lage oberhalb eines Botanischen Gartens kann der Blick ins Grüne schweifen, genauso aber auch über den Atlantischen Ozean. Um diese Aussicht optimal zu nutzen, verglasten die Planer das innen liegende Schwimmbad großflächig: Während der Gast es im geheizten Wasser mit der Gegenstromanlage aufnehmen kann, die dafür sorgt, dass er ein wenig länger braucht, um das 13,5 Meter lange Becken zu durchschwimmen, kann er durch die Panoramafenster hinausschauen und sich noch überlegen, ob er nicht doch lieber in den größeren, außen liegenden Pool mit seinen 250 Quadratmetern springen soll. Der Terrassenbelag aus Natursteinplatten und kleine Pflanzenfelder direkt am Beckenrand, die von Bruchstein- wänden eingefasst sind, erzeugen dort den Eindruck eines naturnahen Badens.

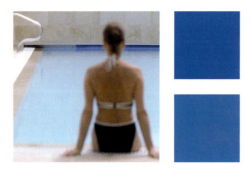

cowley manor | gloucestershire . united kingdom
DESIGN: Ryan de Matos Storey

The spa area at Cowley Manor simulates an enclosed landscape, consisting of two pools. The indoor pool is lined with dark grey, green Welsh slate underneath a lavender meadow, becoming continuous with the surrounding landscaped gardens with groves of maples and Acers, lead from the hotel itself. This rectangular pool lies adjacent to the spa's treatment rooms, changing area, sauna and steam room. Strongly colored roof lights naturally light the spa; the interior pool looks out through a glass wall over the wooded landscape and the outdoor pool. The outdoor pool, heated year round, is situated in a "secret" sunken courtyard with walls of cast stone, natural fractured Cotswold limestone, pigmented concrete softened by Yew hedge and garden of bamboos. This award winning pool complex is a contemporary and contemplative country house hotel.

Das Spa des Cowley Manor mit seinen beiden Pools ist mehr Landschaft als Architektur. Das Schwimmbad im Gebäudeinnern kontrastiert mit dunkelgrünem Schiefer aus Wales zur lavendelfarbenen Wiese, die sich zum Landschaftsgarten des Hotels mit seinen Ahornbäumen ausdehnt. Das Rechteck des Hallenbads grenzt an den Spa-Bereich mit Sauna, Dampfbad und den Behandlungsräumen. Am Tag fällt hier Sonnenlicht durch bunte Deckenfenster. Gleichzeitig überblickt man durch die breite Glasfront den kompletten Außenbereich mit dem Außenpool, der das ganze Jahr über beheizt wird. Er liegt eine Stufe tiefer und etwas versteckt in einem Innenhof, der von einer unregelmäßigen Mauer aus Kunststein, gebrochenem Kalkstein aus Cotswold und Kiesbeton eingefasst wird. Bambus und Eibensträucher lockern das Gesamtbild auf. Der preisgekrönte Pool-Komplex ist beispielhaft für eine zeitgemäße und feinfühlige Integration moderner Architektur in das denkmalgeschützte Ensemble des italienischen Country House Hotels.

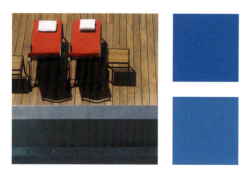

gran hotel la florida | barcelona . spain

DESIGN: Dale Keller, Marta Salafranca

Float from the cool, dark shade of the slate clad spa area out towards the infinity edge of this 37-metre stainless steel pool. The water mirages into the pale blue of the sky, away and over the Mediterranean Sea. Gaze through the slim fingertips of cypress trees, across the murmuring metropolis of Barcelona beneath you. Perched up high on Mount Tibidabo, Gran Hotel La Florida has a commanding position over the city in the provision of luxury lodgings. Completely renovated and sensitively restored, the hotel re-opened in 2003, with this feature pool providing the focus for the outdoor Miramar Bar. Sun loungers sit on terraces of wood decking that step down beneath the pool. Alongside, cool water whispers past in a stainless steel trough, at the base of a high stonewall of rough hewn, end of slab slate and bright white quartz. The refraction of the dazzling southern Spanish sun patterns the stainless steel pool, displaying the shimmering turquoises, and pale verdigris greens of a peacock's fan, clear against the mirror finish of the bright steel. Feel the multitude of smooth rivets bumping gently under your feet whilst your shoulders get a soothing massage from either of the swan-necked high-pressure water jets. A glass guillotine provides protection from the mild winters, keeping the indoor Jacuzzi area available year round.

Das hoch auf dem Mount Tibidabo gelegene Luxushotel ist neben der verspielten Kirche auch von der Stadt aus gut sichtbar. Entsprechend grandios ist der Panoramablick in die umgekehrte Richtung, der sich den Gästen hier oben eröffnet. Diese Aussicht genießt man nicht nur aus den Fenstern bzw. von den Terrassen der Gästezimmer, sondern auch beim Schwimmen. Wer sich aus dem kühlen, dunklen Schatten des in Schiefergrau gehaltenen Wellnessbereichs bis zum Rand des 37 Meter langen, nicht rostenden Stahlpools treiben lässt, schwimmt optisch in Richtung Mittelmeer. Das Wasser vereinigt sich mit dem hellblauen Himmel, der sich über das Meer wölbt. Der einzigartige Pool bildet den Mittelpunkt der außen gelegenen Miramar-Bar. Die Sonnenliegen befinden sich auf Terrassen mit Holzbelag, die unterhalb des Pools verlaufen. Daneben plätschert in einer nicht rostenden Stahlrinne kühles Wasser vorbei, entlang einer hohen Mauer aus Schiefergestein und weißem Quarz. Die Strahlen der Sonne brechen sich in dem Stahlpool, der in den türkisfarbenen und hellen Grüntönen eines Pfauenrads schimmert, die sich klar von dem Stahl abheben. Fühlen Sie die Vielzahl von kleinen Nietverbindungen unter Ihren Füßen, während Ihre Schultern von den Hochdruck-Wasserdüsen massiert werden. Der Jacuzzi-Innenbereich ist durch Glas vor den milden Wintern geschützt und damit ganzjährig verfügbar.

48 | gran hotel la florida

life gallery | athens . greece
DESIGN: Klein Heller, Vasilis Rodatos

Glass is the dominant material of this hotel located in Ekali – a northern suburb of Athens. The transparent building material serves not only as the building casing but was incorporated into other areas of the hotel in a spectacular manner: the entire long side of the swimming pool in the garden is glass. The swimming guests can be observed through this glass wall both above and below the water surface. A second outdoor pool and an indoor pool complete the pool landscape. For those guests requiring additional relaxation, the Ananena Spa offers an assortment of massages and therapeutic mud treatment. The architecture is exceptionally modern and puristic, seldom found in Greece.

Glas ist das dominierende Material dieses Hotelbaus, der in Ekali, einem nördlichen Vorort Athens, liegt. Der transparente Baustoff dient nicht nur als Gebäudehülle, sondern wurde an anderer Stelle des Hotels auf deutlich spektakulärere Weise eingesetzt: Er bildet die Längswand des Swimmingpools im Garten. Durch diese Glaswand hindurch lassen sich nun die Badenden beim Schwimmen beobachten, allerdings nicht nur über der Wasseroberfläche, sondern auch darunter. Ein zweites Außenbecken und ein Innenbecken runden das Badeangebot ab. Wem diese Pools noch nicht genug Entspannung bieten, kann sich im Ananena Spa diverse Massagen oder eine Schlammbehandlung gönnen. Die Architektur ist außerordentlich modern und purististisch, wie man sie in Griechenland selten findet.

crown plaza resort | madeira . portugal

DESIGN: Ricardo Nogueira, Caldeira Silva

The center of attraction at the Crowne Plaza Resort is undoubtedly the immense selection of sports and recuperation activities. In addition to the usual sauna and steam bath, the hotel offers a unique Thalasso Therapy at its "Marine Spa", two squash courts, a kids club, and a diver base. And swimmers will not be disappointed. Large glass fronts in the indoor pool create a fluent transition between indoor and outdoor areas and merge the pool with the garden. Here await two large deep-blue pools, the edges of which optically connect to the ocean beyond. Those who crave the typical feel of saltwater on their skin after this spectacular view will not be disappointed: the pools are filled with saltwater.

Zentraler Anziehungspunkt des Crowne Plaza Resort ist sicherlich das riesige Angebot an Sport- und Erholungsmöglichkeiten. Neben Selbstverständlichkeiten wie Sauna und Dampfbad zählen die Thalassotherapie des „Marine Spa", zwei Squash-Courts, ein Kids-Club und die hoteleigene Tauchbasis zu den Besonderheiten. Auch Badefreunde kommen auf ihre Kosten. Beim Hallenbad schaffen nicht nur große Glasfronten einen fließenden Übergang von innen nach außen, sondern auch das Becken, das sich durch die Fensterfront hindurch in den Garten hinaus fortsetzt. Dort warten zwei große tiefblaue Pools, deren Wasserkante sich optisch direkt mit dem Ozean verbindet. Wer durch diese Aussicht Sehnsucht nach dem typischen Gefühl auf der Haut bekommen hat, das sich nach einem Bad im Meer einstellt, wird nicht enttäuscht: Die Pools sind mit Salzwasser gefüllt.

contemporary minimalistic

banyan tree seychelles | mahé . intendance bay . seychelles
DESIGN: Architrave Design & Planning Co.

Either in the rain forest or lying directly on the beach, from the 36 white villas of the resort, one can see the Indian Ocean and the sandy bay – the epitome of a postcard cliché. Along the sandy beaches, one can even find giant tortoises. Some of the villas enjoy their own private whirlpool and swimming pool. Those who didn't book this luxury will have to content themselves with the main pool, which is nothing less than breathtaking. The freestanding cube is dramatically perched on a steep slope, so guests while swimming can look beyond three sides of the water surface over the Infinity Edge and take in the panoramic view of either the landscape or the ocean. One seems to swim towards the far horizon. After the refreshing water, however, it is strongly recommended to seek the revitalizing effects of a cool drink at the pool bar.

Ob im Regenwald oder direkt am Strand gelegen, von den 47 weißen Villen des Resorts aus blickt man über den Indischen Ozean und die feinsandige Bucht, die hier beim Banyan Tree zu einer der schönsten weltweit gehört. Eingerahmt in Palmen und die für die Seychellen typischen gerundeten Granitblöcke, bietet die Szenerie das reinste Postkartenklischee. Beim Strandspaziergang kann man sogar Riesenschildkröten begegnen. Die meisten der 47 Villen verfügen neben einem eigenen Whirlpool auch über ein eigenes Schwimmbecken zur Erfrischung. Wer mehr als zwei, drei Züge schwimmen möchte, findet im Hauptpool zwei geräumige Becken, die zwar nicht ganz olympische Ausmaße erreichen, sportlichen Ansprüchen aber genügen. Daneben besticht die Anlage vor allem durch ihre Architektur: Als frei stehender Quader liegt der Pool dramatisch an einem steil abfallenden Hang, sodass der Gast beim Baden an drei Seiten der Wasserfläche über die flache Kante hinweg in die Ferne blicken kann – entweder auf die Landschaft oder das Meer. Man scheint geradezu dem Horizont entgegenzuschwimmen.

devi garh | udaipur . india

DESIGN: Gautam Bathia, Navin Gupta, Rajiv Saini

The imposing palatial building, Devi Garh, is perched high over the entrance to the Valley of Udaipur. It was at this place five hundred years ago that the infamous Mogul invasions were successfully averted. And that is hardly any wonder in view of this architecture, radiating its immense self-esteem. Its ocher façade is visible from afar. After a period of restoration spanning several years, Devi Garh was rediscovered as a merging point between the past and the present. Pure luxury still predominates in the palace high over the village, Delwara. The proprietors and designers nevertheless consistently reduced the richness of the building to form and material. Hence, the basin of the Devi Garh Pool and many other areas of Devi Garh have been trimmed with marble. The palace building is optically prioritized by emphasizing simple lines and renouncing the use of ornamentation. The pool is clearly defined as a place for contemplation and peace and is therefore aesthetically united in harmony with the playfully designed façade of the palace and its finely chased pavilions. Despite its prominent location, the pool nevertheless remains a place of tranquil retreat.

Hoch über dem Eingang zum Tal von Udaipur thront der imposante Palastbau Devi Garh. An diesem Ort wurden vor einem halben Jahrtausend die Mogulen-Invasionen gleich mehrmals erfolgreich abgewehrt. Beim Anblick dieser Selbstbewusstsein ausstrahlenden Architektur nimmt das kaum wunder. Die ockergelbe Fassade des Palasts ist bereits weithin sichtbar. Nach mehrjähriger Restaurierung wurde Devi Garh als ein Ort neu entdeckt, an dem Vergangenheit und Zukunft ineinander fließen. Purer Luxus herrscht nach wie vor in dem Palast über dem Dorf Delwara. Die Besitzer und Designer reduzierten den Reichtum des Gebäudes jedoch konsequent auf Form und Material. So ist das Bassin auf einer hoch gelegenen Terrasse des Palastes, wie viele andere Bereiche des Devi Garh, komplett in Marmor eingefasst. Seine klare Form und völliger Verzicht auf schmückende Elemente stehen dem Palastgebäude nicht die Schau. Der Pool grenzt sich klar als Ort der Kontemplation und Ruhe ab und steht dabei ästhetisch in harmonischem Einklang mit der verspielt gestalteten Fassade des Palasts oder den fein ziselierten Pavillons. Trotz seiner prominenten Lage bleibt der Pool so immer irgendwie ein Rückzugsort.

grand hyatt mumbai | mumbai . india
DESIGN: Bilkey Linas Design, Skidmore & Owens & Merrill of London

Grand Hyatt Mumbai is a landmark – in the middle of the city. Due to its convenient location on the main traffic lines, guests can reach the international airport in only 20 minutes, the booming Bandra-Kurla bank center in five minutes. The complex is situated on a site covering almost 10 acres and offers more that 500 rooms and suites. In conjunction with the integrated shopping mall and entertainment center, the entire hotel complex almost constitutes a small city within a city. Those seeking relaxation will find it at Club Oasis. After a vigorous workout on the tennis courts or in the fitness center, the spa offers exotic massages or aromatherapy and a cooling dip in the pool. The post-modern hotel façade, adorned with different light stone slates, is reflected on the surface of the water. The paved floor around the pool mirrors the creative theme of the façade and is also arranged in stripes. The dominance of stone corresponds to the urban setting of the hotel.

Das Grand Hyatt Mumbai ist eine Landmarke – mitten in der Stadt. Durch seine verkehrsgünstige Lage erreicht der Gast den internationalen Flughafen in zwanzig, das boomende Bankenviertel Bandra-Kurla in fünf Minuten. Der Komplex erstreckt sich über ein Gelände von vier Hektar und bietet weit über 500 Zimmer und Suiten sowie einen eigenen Appartementkomplex für Gäste, die eine Bleibe für mehr als einen Monat suchen. Zusammen mit einer mehrstöckigen Shopping Mall und einem Entertainment Center bildet die Anlage fast eine kleine Stadt in der Stadt. Wer Entspannung sucht, wird im Club Oasis fündig: Nachdem man sich auf den Tennisplätzen oder im Fitnesscenter verausgabt hat, kann man sich im Spa eine exotische Massage oder eine Aromatherapie gönnen oder aber zum Abkühlen in einen der Pools springen. Im Wasser des privaten Pools der Appartementanlage spiegelt sich die postmoderne Fassade mit ihren Streifen aus unterschiedlich hellen Steinplatten. Der gepflasterte Boden um den Pool herum nimmt das gestalterische Thema der Fassade auf und ist ebenfalls in Streifen gegliedert. Die Dominanz des Materials Stein entspricht der städtischen Lage des Hotels. Im Hauptpool lockern quadratische, mit Bäumen bepflanzte Platten in den Ecken und als Inseln die Wasserfläche auf und spenden zudem Schatten.

casa del mar | corsica . france

DESIGN: Bodin & Associés, Carol Marcellesi

Right from the first glance, the fascinating jagged coastline of the Gulf of Porto Vecchio in southeastern Corsica is wooed by the various Mediterranean blue hues at all times of the day. The Hotel Casa del mar harmonizes with the color of the sky and the sea in the bright, warm wood with which the entire building was faced. It opened in 2004, taking on an elegant silvery gleam and an elegant touch over the Bay of Porto Vecchio. Both the over-sized glass front of the main building and the terraces of the twenty suites and rooms of the hotel face the ocean. Between the hotel and the bay, one sees the 25 meter-wide pool, surrounded by a Mediterranean garden. The pool is situated a few steps above the beach like a huge mirror, hardly brighter than the sea. The sun-beds in light grey anticipating the sundeck colors corresponding to the Corsican stone. The square, bright colored sunshades float light as paper airplanes over the pool emphasizing the harmonious charisma of the ambience.

Der Golf von Porto Vecchio im Südosten von Korsika fasziniert auf den ersten Blick durch seine schroffe Küstenlinie, die zu jeder Tageszeit von den verschiedensten Schattierungen mediterranen Blaus umschmeichelt wird. Das Hotel Casa del mar harmoniert mit der Farbe des Himmels und des Meeres in hellem, warmem Holz, mit dem das gesamte Gebäude verkleidet wurde. Es wird wenige Sommer dauern, bis das 2004 eröffnete Haus einen elegant silbrigen Schimmer annimmt und noch eine Spur eleganter über der Bucht von Porto Vecchio thront. Nicht nur die überdimensionale Glasfront des Hauptgebäudes, auch die Terrassen der 20 Suiten und Zimmer im Hotel Casadelmar sind dem Meer zugewandt. Zwischen Hotel und Bucht sieht man von dort den 25 Meter breiten Pool, umgeben von einem mediterranen Garten. Wie ein überdimensionaler Spiegel, kaum heller als das Meer, liegt der Pool wenige Stufen über dem Strand. Die Sonnenliegen in hellem Grau nehmen schon jetzt die spätere Farbe des Sonnendecks vorweg und korrespondieren mit korsischem Gestein. Leicht wie Papierflieger schweben die quadratischen hellen Sonnenschirme über dem Poolbereich und unterstreichen die harmonische Ausstrahlung dieses Ambientes.

maricel | mallorca . spain

DESIGN: Xavier Claramont

The Maricel, meaning sea (mar) and sky (cel), was built as a hotel to accommodate guests at the Marivent (sea and wind), the former royal Mallorcan palace across the bay. The recent complete renovation of this imposing property consists of 29 rooms out of 60 original ones; and it has retained the original neo-classical exterior. The mellow sandstone of the columns and arches extends down to the pool and terrace. The modernist curves and angles of the pool terrace are softened through the broken shadows thrown by the needles of a dominant, gnarled and ancient pine. The deep blue of the still pool mirrors the sky, providing a subtle textural contrast to the multi-faceted movement of the sea beyond the pool's infinity edge. Spa treatments can be taken poolside, in the privacy of one of the screened arches that vault under the hotel itself. The hotel and pool sit in a small bay with two rocky promontories on either side. The pool drops off sheer into the bay; yachts glide from the distant horizon to berth just beneath you at the hotel's own jetty.

Das Maricel – der Name bedeutet Meer (mar) und Himmel (cel) – wurde gebaut, um Gäste des Marivent (Meer und Wind), des früheren mallorquinischen Königspalasts jenseits der Bucht, zu beherbergen. Bei der vor kurzem durchgeführten vollständigen Renovierung dieses imposanten Anwesens wurde die Anzahl der Zimmer von ursprünglich 60 auf 29 reduziert und die originale neoklassizistische Fassade beibehalten. Die Säulen und Bogen aus zart gefärbtem Sandstein erstrecken sich bis zum Pool und der dazugehörigen Terrasse hinunter. Die modernistischen Winkel und Ecken der Poolterrasse werden durch die Schattenspiele einer riesigen, knorrigen alten Kiefer abgemildert. Im tiefen Blau des reglosen Wassers spiegelt sich der Himmel wider und bildet einen feinen Kontrast zu den vielfältigen Bewegungen des Meeres jenseits des Beckenrands. Direkt neben dem Pool, abgeschirmt durch die gemauerten Bogen, die sich unter dem Hotel befinden, kann man sich mit Wellnessbehandlungen verwöhnen lassen. Hotel und Pool liegen in einer kleinen Bucht; auf beiden Seiten befinden sich zwei Felsvorsprünge. Der Pool verläuft direkt in die Bucht, am fernen Horizont sieht man Jachten dahingleiten, die dann im hoteleigenen Jachthafen vor Anker gehen.

chedi muscat | oman

DESIGN: Jean-Michel Gathy & Yasuhiro Koichi

On the outskirts of Oman's capital, Muscat, lies The Chedi, a complex ensemble of radiating white buildings, reminiscent of Alhambra if it weren't for its modern architecture. Inner courtyards offer an intricate system of ponds; a water garden sparkles in front of the restaurant. But the hotel is not by any means introverted. All rooms offer a fascinating view over either the azure-blue Indian Ocean or nearby mountains. A private beach 350 meters long also belongs to the hotel. For those children of nature who are more comfortably inclined, the hotel also has two pools. One offers quiet relaxation – and is therefore only accessible to adults – while the other pool presents a great playing opportunity for kids. The design does not emphasize oriental splendor but modern functionality. Canvas is suspended over the water to provide some protection from the searing midday sun.

Am Rande von Omans Hauptstadt Muscat liegt das Chedi, ein komplexes Ensemble strahlend weißer Gebäude, das den Betrachter an die Alhambra erinnern könnte, wäre da nicht die moderne Architektur. Die Innenhöfe warten mit einem verschlungenen System von Teichen auf, vor dem Restaurant liegt ein Wassergarten. Doch die Anlage ist keineswegs introvertiert, vielmehr bieten alle Zimmer eine faszinierende Aussicht, entweder auf den azurblauen Indischen Ozean oder auf die nahe gelegenen Berge. Ein Privatstrand von 350 Metern Länge gehört ebenfalls zum Hotel. Wen es nach dem Bad im Meer wieder ins Süßwasser zieht, kann in den beiden Hotelpools schwimmen, ohne den Blickkontakt zum Ozean aufgeben zu müssen. Wie bei der gesamten Anlage und den Zimmern haben die Architekten auch bei den Pools auf moderne Sachlichkeit gesetzt und Orientalisches auf Details beschränkt. Schutz vor der starken Mittagssonne bietet das quer über das Wasser gespannte Segeltuch.

four seasons resort bali at sayan | bali . indonesia
DESIGN: John Heah

Four Season Resort Bali at Sayan with its rice terraces adapts its three floored, terrace-like facility very harmoniously into the green hilly countryside near Ubud, but still seems to be absolutely futuristic. From afar, the round pool in the uppermost hotel extension appears to be an UFO, a former flying saucer, which filled-up with rainwater after landing and now mirrors the blueness of the sky. Underneath, the restaurant and lobby nestle in; the freestanding villas and suites appear rather inconspicuous on the Ayung River valley cliffs. They nearly disappear into the luxuriant green of the palm groves and trees. Perhaps the guest might initially be a bit disappointed that the above-mentioned roof pool is purely decoration and not suited for bathing; however, the two-level swimming pool situated a couple of floors below offers an exceedingly attractive alternative. Both pools, located on top of one another, cuddle into the natural form of the rocks. Over the pool edge, one peruses the course of the Ayung River, seeming to act as a continuation of the hotel pool. Both pools are framed in a deck made of noble woods and, toward the cliff, in walls of light stone.

Von weitem sieht das runde Bassin auf dem Dach des elliptischen Hotelgebäudes wie ein Ufo aus, das sich nach der Landung mit Regenwasser gefüllt hat und nun das Blau des Himmels spiegelt. Darunter schmiegen sich Restaurant und Lobby sowie die Suiten und frei stehenden Villen eher unscheinbar an das Hochufer des Ayung-River-Tals. Sie verschwinden beinahe im üppigen Grün der Palmen und Bäume. Vielleicht ist der Gast zunächst etwas enttäuscht, dass das oben genannte Dachbecken reine Zierde und zum Baden ungeeignet ist. Doch der zweistufige, ein paar Etagen darunter liegende Swimmingpool ist eine überaus attraktive Alternative. Die beiden übereinander liegenden Bassins verlaufen in der natürlichen Form des Felsens. Über die Kanten der Bassins blickt man in die kleinen Stromschnellen des Ayung River, der wie die natürliche Fortsetzung der Hotelpools wirkt. Eingefasst sind die beiden Poolbecken von einem Deck aus edlen Hölzern und zum Felsen hin mit Mauern aus hellem Stein.

alila ubud | bali . indonesia
DESIGN: Kerry Hill Architects

A simple pool in a dramatic location. A dark, emerald-green rectangle reflecting the tropical sun perches on a spur, bounded by the infinite greens that make up the landscape of central Bali. Alila, the Sanskrit word for "surprise", is a luxurious hotel a few minutes through the terraced rice fields from Ubud, the island's cultural capital. The hotel and pool were designed by Kerry Hill architects and opened in 1996, a time when infinity edge pools were indeed a surprise. By night, oil lamps light the sweeping stone stairs leading to the pool. Steep slopes drop off either side, down to tributaries of the Ayung River. The closeness to nature is tantalizing – the infinity edge of the pool seems to lap up against the jungle itself. Singing birds, chattering monkeys and the sashaying of the palm fronds in the breeze are the sounds to accompany the serenity of the pool itself. Appearing to float in the shallow end of the pool is a large arrangement fragrant jasmine, the hotel's signature flower; it is a delicate contrast to the depth of the dark water surrounding it. No surprise that this pool is an award winner – appearing on the cover of Travel & Leisure magazine's Top 50 Pools edition.

Ein schlichter Pool in dramatischer Umgebung. Ein dunkles, smaragd-grünes Rechteck spiegelt das Glitzern der tropischen Sonnenstrahlen, die vom unendlichen Grün der Vegetation im Inneren Balis eingerahmt werden. Das Alila Ubud – „Alila" ist Sanskrit und bedeutet ‚Überraschung' – ist ein Luxushotel, das man in nur wenigen Minuten Fahrt durch die Reisterrassenfelder von Ubud aus erreicht. Das Hotel und auch der Pool wurden von Kerry Hill entworfen und 1996 eröffnet, zu einer Zeit, als „Infinity Pools" noch eine architektonische Überraschung waren. Abends ist der Weg über die geschwungenen Steintreppen zum Pool von Öllampen gesäumt. Auf beiden Seiten bricht die Böschung steil ab zu den Nebenflüssen des Ayung River. Die Unmittelbarkeit der Natur macht den Reiz dieser Umgebung aus – an seinem Ende berührt der Pool den Dschungel. Vogelstimmen, das Geplapper von Affen und das Rascheln der Palmwedel sind der akustische Rahmen für dieses überirdische Ambiente. Ein großes Bukett von wohlriechendem Jasmin, der Blume aus dem Signet des Hotels, scheint am flacheren Ende des Pools auf der Wasseroberfläche zu treiben. Ein feiner Kontrast zur dunklen Tiefe des Wassers, das es umgibt. Es nimmt kaum wunder, dass dieser Pool preisgekrönt ist – und beispielhaft eine Titelstory des Reisemagazins „Travel & Leisure" über die 50 schönsten Pools der Welt illustrierte.

the lalu | sun-moon lake . taiwan
DESIGN: Kerry Hill Architects

Guests of The Lalu are greeted with a breathtaking view of spectacular jade-green mountains and Sun Moon Lake, the largest freshwater lake in Taiwan. This unusual name is attributed to the shape of the lake: the northern end resembles the sun and the southern end a crescent moon. Because of the location in the midst of a green and lush natural environment, designers of the hotel opted to implement severe and restrained architectural forms. And thus the pool was designed not with formal frivolity but as a simple rectangle – 60 meters in length – providing guests with a tranquil opportunity to swim long and leisurely laps. Further relaxation either before or after a dip in the pool can be found in the Spa, where green tea is used as therapy for the body.

Den Gästen des Lalu bietet sich eine wunderbare Aussicht auf jadegrüne Berge und den Sun Moon Lake, den größten Süßwassersee Taiwans. Seinen ungewöhnlichen Namen verdankt der See seiner Form: Das nördliche Ende ähnelt der Sonne, das südliche dagegen einer Mondsichel. Auf die Lage inmitten der üppig grünen Natur reagierten die Planer des Hotels mit einer strengen, zurückhaltenden Architektur. So verzichteten sie auch beim Pool auf formale Spielereien und konzipierten ihn als einfaches Rechteck, das sich allerdings 60 Meter in die Länge streckt und damit die Chance bietet, in aller Ruhe angenehm lange Bahnen zu ziehen. Für noch weiter gehende Entspannung empfiehlt sich vor oder nach dem Schwimmen auch ein Besuch im Spa, wo der Körper mit grünem Tee behandelt wird.

the legian & the club at the legian | bali . indonesia

DESIGN: Ibrahim Jaya, Jaya Associates

The Indian Ocean delivers wave after powerful wave on to the steeply sloping, soft sand of Seminyak beach in front of The Legian hotel on Bali's west coast. Potentially useful to surfers, although they prefer the conditions further south at Uluwatu, the strong cross current makes an ocean dip a slightly nervy experience for the uninitiated. No wonder that the hotel's two-tiered pool proves so popular with guests. Symmetrically laid out, a graceful entry is assured by the shallow steps at either end of the pool; taking one physically to the edge of the pool and mentally to the ocean's edge. All around the manicured lawns surrounding the pool, there are hardwood loungers in the shade of tall palms. In addition to this, fresh towels, chilled facial clothes and iced water on a tray with a ubiquitous, sweet smelling frangipani flower are offered here as well. For more privacy, the villas at the hotel's adjacent Club complex have an exclusive 10 meter pool for individual use.

Die mächtigen Wellen des Indischen Ozeans schlagen gegen den steil abfallenden, weichen Sandstrand von Seminyak Beach vor dem Hotel The Legian an der Westküste von Bali. Die starke Gegenströmung mag für Surfer geeignet sein (obwohl diese weiter südlich, in Uluwatu, bessere Bedingungen vorfinden), für unerfahrene Schwimmer ist sie jedoch eine nervenaufreibende Erfahrung. Kein Wunder also, dass sich der auf zwei Ebenen verteilte Hotelpool bei den Gästen großer Beliebtheit erfreut. Symmetrisch angelegt sorgen die flachen Stufen zu beiden Seiten des Pools für einen eleganten Einstieg. Bequem lässt es sich mit den Füßen im Wasser des oberen Pools planschen, während man die Brecher am Rande des Ozeans beobachtet. Überall auf dem gepflegten Rasen, der den Pool umgibt, findet man Sonnenliegen aus Hartholz im Schatten hoher Palmen. Hier werden dem Gast sofort frische Handtücher, kühle Gesichtstücher und Eiswasser auf einem Tablett gebracht – dekoriert mit einer süß duftenden Jasminblüte. Wer allerdings mehr Privatheit sucht, sollte sich für eine der Villen in der angrenzenden Clubanlage entscheiden, die mit einem eigenen Pool von 10 Metern Länge zur exklusiven Nutzung aufwarten.

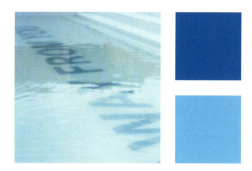

deseo | playa del carmen . mexico

DESIGN: Manuel Cervantes, Moisés Ison, José Sánchez, Central de Arquitectura

The DJ sits crossed legged, in front of his turntables, resting on the wood deck with the music flowing as the water flows. His sounds set the scene for the glamorous crowd lounging on the giant day beds – tanned limbs moving against white covers. Surveying all is the silent, black and white movie projected up onto an end wall. The pool has its own motto, Away From You, incorporated in the bottom surface. Mexican artist Silvia Gruner undertook the in situ work; the motto coming from her video installation, of the same name; it is a story of isolation and individuality, of a beautiful swimmer who sets out to cross a pool but never reaches the other side; however, this pool has borders but the relief from the bright sun of Playa del Carmen and the chill out music, truly isolate you in space. Away From You is at once thought provoking and true. Here, one storey up from the street life of Playa del Carmen, one is really away from everything. But not the party, the one in which everyone wants to be seen. Deseo Pool and Lounge provide the most audacious piece of style along the whole Mayan Rivieria.

Gleich neben dem DJ zelebrieren Mixer einer anderen Art ihre Kunst unter dem einfachen Glasdach der Bar. Über allem stumme Szenen eines Schwarzweißfilms, an eine der Außenwände projiziert. Der Pool hat sein eigenes Motto: „Away from you" – fern von dir, auf dem Grund des Pools von der mexikanischen Künstlerin Silvia Gruner festgeschrieben. Der Satz stammt aus einer ihrer Videoinstallationen. Die Geschichte handelt von Isolation und Individualität. Ein schöner Körper stößt sich am Beckenrand ab, um den Pool zu durchqueren, kommt jedoch nie am anderen Ende an. Solche Probleme hat der Gast des Deseo nicht. Der Pool ist einzig und allein für eine kleine, belebende Erfrischung gedacht, sei es von der intensiven Sonne Mexikos oder den einschläfernden Chill-out-Sounds der Musik. „Away from you" ist provokant und zugleich wahr. Nur ein Stockwerk über der lebendigen Szenerie auf den Straßen von Playa del Carmen ist man hier weit, weit weg von allem – außer von dieser grandiosen Party, auf der es einzig und allein um sehen und gesehen werden geht. Pool und Lounge des Deseo sind eines der mutigsten und frechsten Ambiente der ganzen Riviera Maya in Yucatan.

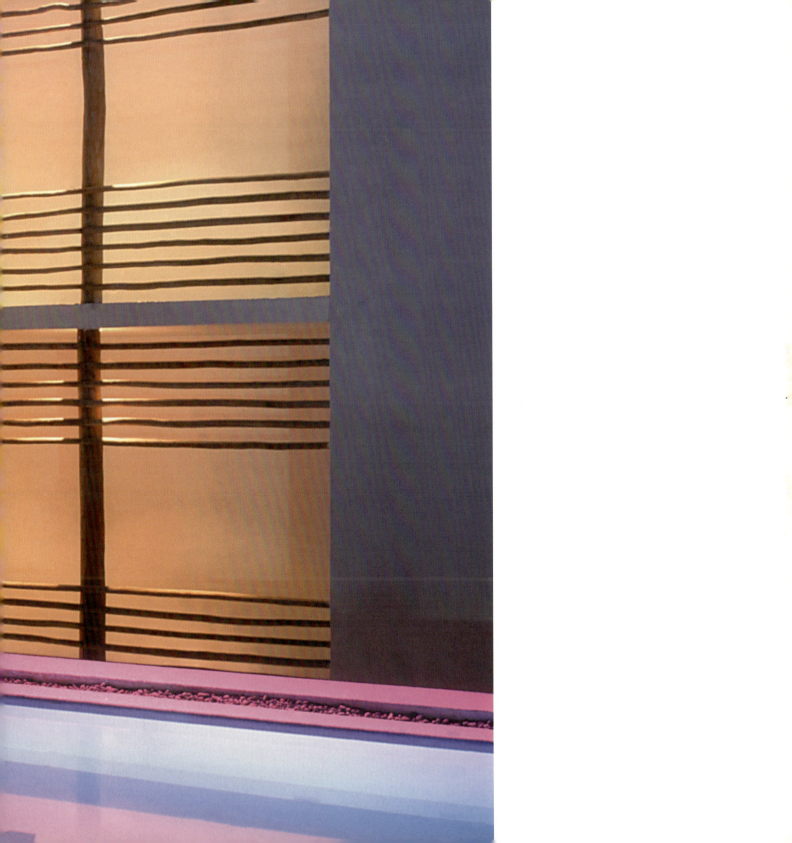

ksar char-bagh | marrakech . morocco
DESIGN: Nicole Grandsire & Patrick Le Villair

The pool at this hotel offers an exceptionally unique swimming experience. An elongated basin, bordered on two sides by sturdy palm trees, is directed towards a majestic, palatial-like building. Bathers swim towards the main portal of the building, which is reflected in the water. Although it is easy to imagine being in a historic complex, the hotel is new and opened in 2002. Not only does the swimming pool offer physical regeneration, but a Hammam, furnished in the Ottoman Style, can also be found here. The entire hotel complex consists of a series of connected room cells that provide a succession and penetration of interior and exterior rooms, creating a fascinating and varied transit through the ensemble.

Ein außergewöhnliches Badeerlebnis bietet das Schwimmbad dieses Hotels. Ein lang gestrecktes Bassin, das auf zwei Seiten von wuchtigen Palmen gesäumt wird, läuft geradewegs auf ein imposantes, palastähnliches Gebäude zu. Die Badenden schwimmen dem Hauptportal des Bauwerks entgegen, das sich im Wasser spiegelt. Man wähnt sich in einer historischen Anlage, das Hotel wurde jedoch neu errichtet und erst im Jahr 2003 eröffnet. Der körperlichen Regeneration dient nicht nur das Schwimmbecken, sondern auch ein Hammam, der im ottomanischen Stil ausgestattet ist. Die Gesamtanlage setzt sich aus einem Gefüge von Raumzellen zusammen, das in der Abfolge und Durchdringung von Innen- und Außenräumen einen abwechslungsreichen Gang durch das Ensemble ermöglicht.

verana | puerto vallarta . mexico
DESIGN: Heinz Legler, Veronique Lièvre

Journeying to Verana is an adventure in itself: After a car drive from Puerto Vallarta to Boca de Tomatlan, the last village accessible by car, the trek continues by boat to Yelapa, where donkeys await to bear visitors and luggage to the secluded resort. The exotic grounds nestle in a clearing in the jungle on the crest of a hill, and the resort consists of only six guest cottages, accommodating a maximum of 16 guests – a truly private hideaway. The resort was planned by the renowned Los Angeles scenic designer, Heinz Legler, and it is therefore no wonder that the guest feels as if he were living in a film set. Because the central theme here is centered on life submerged in nature, the planners forwent naturally sweeping curves when designing the pool. Instead, the sharply formed L identifies the pool as a distinct artistic element. It is filled with spring water cascading down from nearby mountains. Although the pool is centrally located on the resort grounds, it offers a breathtaking panoramic view over the ocean. Only two palm trees seem to vie for attention in the foreground - as if a set director had forgotten them there.

Die Anreise könnte abenteuerlicher nicht sein: Nach einer Autofahrt von Puerto Vallarta nach Boca de Tomatlan, dem letzten Ort, der mit dem Auto erreichbar ist, geht es mit dem Boot weiter nach Yelapa, wo Esel warten, um den Gast und sein Gepäck in das völlig abgelegene Resort zu bringen. Die Anlage schmiegt sich in eine Lichtung im Dschungel, die auf einem Hügel liegt. Sie besteht aus nur sechs Gästehäusern, die zusammen maximal 16 Gäste gleichzeitig beherbergen können – privater geht es kaum. Geplant wurde sie von dem in Los Angeles lebenden Bühnenbildner Heinz Legler, und so nimmt es nicht wunder, dass der Gast sich hier fühlen kann wie in einem Filmset. Da das Leben mitten in der Natur hier die zentrale Rolle spielt, verzichteten die Planer bei der Gestaltung des Pools darauf, natürlich geschwungene Formen einzusetzen. Als scharf geschnittenes L ist er stattdessen deutlich als künstliches Element zu erkennen. Gespeist wird er mit Quellwasser aus den nahe gelegenen Bergen. Obwohl der Pool ungefähr in der Mitte der Anlage liegt, bietet er einen Panoramablick über den Ozean; lediglich zwei Palmen schieben sich in den Vordergrund – als hätte der Requisiteur sie dort abgestellt.

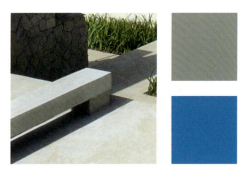

the balé | bali . indonesia
DESIGN: Antony Lui, Karl Princic

The complex consists of only 20 guesthouses, ensuring exclusiveness. Because of the close arrangement of the buildings, however, an urban setting was almost created with alleys, narrow passages, and small cobbled areas between the pavilions. Nevertheless, the privacy of guests is guaranteed despite the crowded building style. Every pavilion has its own private garden that is slightly raised from the public room on the other side, alleviating the need for a wall. The central element here is an elongated swimming pool, which begins practically at the bathroom door and reaches to the edge of the garden where water flows over the Infinity-Edge. A bed of lush sedge grass borders one side of the basin, and a path of light natural stone tiles fringes the other. The interplay of modern western and traditional Asian forms, of hard and soft materials, of light and shadow, of openness and seclusion creates a pleasant place of almost contemplative tranquility.

Die Anlage besteht aus nur 20 Gästehäusern, wodurch für Exklusivität gesorgt ist. In der dichten Anordnung der Gebäude entstand jedoch eine beinahe städtische Struktur mit Gassen, Wegen und steinernen Plätzen zwischen den Pavillons. Die Privatsphäre der Gäste ist trotz der dichten Bauweise garantiert. Zu jedem Pavillon gehört ein eigener, abgeschlossener Garten, der gegenüber dem öffentlichen Raum leicht erhöht liegt, sodass es nicht nötig ist, ihn vollständig mit Mauern zu umgeben. Das zentrale Element dort ist ein lang gezogenes Wasserbecken, das unmittelbar vor den Türen des Badezimmers beginnt und bis zum Rand des Gartens reicht, wo das Wasser über die flache Kante hinweg nach unten plätschert. Auf einer Seite fasst ein Beet mit üppigem Schilfgras das Bassin ein, auf der anderen Seite ein Pfad aus hellen Natursteinplatten. Das Zusammenspiel von westlich-modernen und traditionellen asiatischen Formen, von harten und weichen Materialien, von Licht und Schatten, von Offenheit und Geschlossenheit ergibt einen angenehmen, beinahe kontemplativen Ort.

bedarra island | north queensland . australia
DESIGN: Engelen Moore

Off the northeast coast of Australia lies a small island on which to take a vacation in total seclusion. Named after the island, the resort is comprised of 16 villas, nestled as pavilions in the forest and distributed throughout the extensive grounds. Large wood and glass surfaces characterize their appearance; modern bungalow architecture creates open and generous living areas and takes full advantage of the spectacular view. The wooden floor inside the pavilion extends out onto the patio, establishing a smooth transition between interior and exterior areas. On the terrace, guests can slip into a small pool and – while floating in the water - gaze through the treetops at the ocean beyond. The pool is tiled with uniquely bright blue tiles, creating a cool and refreshing impression even before diving into the clear water. A soothing background noise is provided by the torrent of water splashing into the pool.

Vor der Nordostküste Australiens liegt eine kleine Insel, auf der es sich in vollkommener Zurückgezogenheit Urlaub machen lässt. Zu dem Resort, das den gleichen Namen trägt wie die Insel, gehören nur 16 Villen, die sich – als Pavillons in den Wald eingefügt – über ein weitläufiges Gelände verteilen. Große Holz- und Glasflächen bestimmen ihr Erscheinungsbild; die moderne Bungalow-Architektur, die ein offenes Wohnen ermöglicht, stellt sich ganz in den Dienst einer maximalen Aussicht. Der Übergang von innen nach außen ist fließend, denn der Holzboden im Inneren der Pavillons setzt sich jeweils auch auf der Terrasse fort. Von dort kann der Gast in einen kleinen Pool gleiten und, während er im Wasser liegt, durch Baumwipfel hindurch aufs Meer schauen. Das besonders leuchtende Blau der Fliesen, mit denen der Pool ausgekleidet ist, erzeugt einen kühlen, erfrischenden Eindruck, noch bevor man überhaupt eingetaucht ist. In einem breiten Schwall ergießt sich das Wasser ins Becken und schafft dadurch eine beruhigende Geräuschkulisse.

estalagem da ponta do sol | madeira . portugal

DESIGN: Oliveira Tiago

This hotel is a renovation of an old quinta, situated on a cliff on the south coast of Madeira; it is a visual escape that blends between the contrasts of the rock lined coast and the natural landscape. This contemporary minimalist pool extends itself into the ocean, inviting guests to float over the sea and to a luxurious view. Estalagem da Ponta do Sol was born out of its site, reflecting its context within the design; the terraced hills and mountains speak of the pool's height, creating a harmony between nature and architecture, where the water blends invisibly into the horizon.

Das Hotel entstand aus einer renovierten ehemaligen Quinta und liegt auf einer Klippe an der Südküste Madeiras. Es fügt sich in die natürliche Landschaft mit der Felsenküste ein. Der zeitgenössische, minimalistisch gehaltene Pool scheint sich bis ins Meer zu erstrecken und gibt dadurch den Gästen das Gefühl, auf dem Ozean zu treiben. Estalagem da Ponta do Sol entstand aus der Landschaft heraus, die sich im Design widerspiegelt; aus den terrassierten Hügeln und Bergen ergab sich die hohe Lage des Pools. Es entsteht eine Harmonie zwischen Natur und Architektur, bei der das Wasserbecken unmerklich mit dem Horizont verschmilzt.

hillside su hotel | antalaya . turkey
DESIGN: Eren Talu

To the right, one gazes over snow covered peaks – to the left the broad Bay of Antalya. One anticipates the picturesque fisher village there in the distance, which was still crouched sleepily at the rocky coastline until a few years ago. It is now hemmed by a skyline of skyscrapers, which one desires to inspect more closely. From the perspective of a terrycloth-white daybed – who would have thought that this fabric could ever have become so posh – at the Hillside Su hotel pool, this scene seems almost a bit mundane. The pool is 56 meters long and a few laps wide. One has the choice between two long rows of brilliant white recliners under strictly lined-up, plaited sunshades on both sides of the elongated pool. With cool sounds, acoustically perfect over and under water, here is the place to relax one's soul.

Zur Rechten blickt man auf schneebedeckte Gipfel – zur Linken auf die weite Bucht von Antalya. Dort in der Ferne ahnt man den Hafen des pittoresken Fischerdorfs, das vor wenigen Jahrzehnten noch verschlafen an der Felsenküste kauerte. Jetzt ist es umsäumt von einer Skyline von Wolkenkratzern, die man auch nicht näher betrachten möchte. Aus dem Blickwinkel eines frotteeweißen Daybeds – wer hätte gedacht, dass dieser Stoff jemals todschick sein kann – am Pool des Hillside Su Hotels wirkt diese Szenerie schon fast ein wenig mondän. 56 Meter ist das Becken lang und wenige Bahnen breit. Wer den Poolbereich betritt, wird von einem überdimensionalen Spiegel am Eingang geradezu gedrängt, noch eine schnelle Korrektur der Körperhaltung vorzunehmen. Dann hat man die Wahl zwischen zwei langen Reihen strahlend weißer Liegen unter streng aufgereihten, geflochtenen Sonnenschirmen an beiden Seiten des lang gestreckten Beckens. Ein DJ an der Poolbar sorgt für Musik. Bei coolen Sounds, die über wie unter Wasser die Situation akustisch vervollkommnen, trifft man hier die Upperclass aus Istanbul.

amankila | bali . indonesia
DESIGN: Edward Tuttle

Located on the steep, jungled slopes of east Bali, a view of the Lombok Strait from the Amankila's airy lobby is captivating. Drawn to the vista seen below, the three cascading blue pools defining the property becoming visible. The drop is precipitous, also experienced physically and conceptually. Evocative of the rice terraces, synonymous of Bali, the pool arrangement also refers to the royal water palaces; found in this part known as "Old Bali". The three pools are connected by a series of symmetrical steps at either end, like the grand staircase in a stately home, with a very clean style. The straight edges and simple lines are softened by the addition of intricate, hand-carved wooden wall hangings, numerous plants and hedges. Rattan furniture and coconut shell tables are shadowed by hand made umbrellas. Each terrace features good-sized bales, pavilions, open-sided and covered with thatch. For even more privacy, many of the 34 suites have their own pools and for those a little more active or social; there is also the property's largest pool at the Beach Club in a shaded grove of palms and frangipani. The ultimate experience at the Amankila is to take in the view, being serenaded simultaneously by the calming harmonies of the gamlan players and the cooling sound of water falling from one pool to the other.

Das Amankila liegt auf einem von üppiger Tropenvegetation bewachsenen Hügel im Osten Balis. Von der offenen Lobby reicht der Blick bei klarem Wetter über die Klippen und den tiefblauen Ozean bis zur Nachbarinsel Lombok. Eine breite Steintreppe nach unten entfernt, sticht einem das Blau der drei abgestuften Pools ins Auge. Die drei Becken sind nach unten versetzt jeweils kleiner, wodurch eine Perspektive entsteht, die in ihrer Tiefe überzeichnet wirkt. Vorbild waren die balinesischen Reisterrassen. Die Anlage erinnert an die königlichen Wasserpaläste, die im Osten Balis ihren Ursprung haben. Die drei Pools sind an jedem Ende durch eine Reihe symmetrischer Stufen wie in einer Schlosstreppe verbunden. Scharfe Kanten und allzu gerade Linien werden durch handgeschnitzte Holzverkleidungen, zahlreiche Hängepflanzen und Hecken aufgelockert. Rattanmöbel und Tische aus Kokosnussschalen stehen im Schatten von balinesischen Schirmen. Jede Terrasse verfügt über einen großzügig dimensionierten „bale", einen nach allen Seiten offenen Pavillon mit einem so genannten „alang-alang"-Strohdach. Ein intimeres Badevergnügen bieten die privaten Pools, die zu den 34 Suiten gehören. Sportliche Gäste werden jedoch den größten Pool bevorzugen, der zum Beach Club des Amankila gehört und von Palmen und Frangipani-Pflanzen umsäumt ist.

rooftop pools

adelphi | melbourne . australia
DESIGN: Dentor Corker Marshall Group

The Adelphi, erected by the Australian architects Denton Corker, Marshall Group from a converted warehouse, relies on strong effects achieved through accentuated details. The guest rooms, as with the entire architecture, are kept emphatically reduced in form and color; the architecture and furnishings are designed with strict geometry. The hotel radiates abstractness reminiscent of Mondrian's paintings. This designed coolness demands a counterbalance that awakens one's fantasy and emotions: the breathtaking Adelphi rooftop pool. Framed in the primary colors of red, yellow and blue, and cubes in the highest storey nested on top of each other, the elongated pool is located on the roof of the high-rise. Seemingly merely temporarily placed there, it looms a bit over the building and ends in free space high up, over Flinders Lane. The swimmer discovers its exciting effect upon reaching the glassed end of the pool, sees and feels the abyss of the building-canyon underneath. Filigree braces afford the construction less optical stability than one might wish for at that certain moment, emphasizing the daringness of this design even more.

Nichts für Menschen mit Höhenangst. Das auf Stahlträgern gestützte Schwimmbad des Adelphi ragt rund 3 Meter über die Dachkante hinaus. Aber damit nicht genug. Die Architekten der Denton Corker Marshall Group in Melbourne setzten genau an dieses überragende Ende des kubischen Gebildes einen Glasboden. Wer also bis an den äußeren Rand des immerhin 25 Meter langen – und nur 2,5 Meter breiten – Bassins schwimmt, kann durch das Wasser die Konturen der neun Etagen tiefer parkenden Autos am Rand der Flinders Lane erkennen. So verwegen die filigrane und in den Farben Rot, Gelb und Blau gehaltene Konstruktion bei ihrem Anblick auch wirken mag, so bewährt hat sich der Entwurf in der Praxis. Als Teil eines Fitness- und Spaareals in den obersten Etagen des ehemaligen Lagerhauses bietet das Adelphi damit nicht nur ein Planschbecken, sondern genügt auch den Wünschen von sportlichen Schwimmern. Und das auf äußerst engem Raum.

park hotel chennai | chennai . india
DESIGN: Hirsh, Bedner & Associates

The pool on the roof of The Park Chennai is more than just a pool. Hotel management has created a unique setting that not only offers guests a relaxing opportunity to swim but serves as a venue for culinary events. The pool and the adjoining restaurant "Aqua" merge into a multi-functional unit. A fabulous view of the city greets guests at a barbecue party. Large day beds are enticingly comfortable for lounging around in, and not only do they provide protection from the blazing sun, but when the curtains are closed, occupants are screened from the prying eyes of other guests. Enhancing the distinctive atmosphere is the intriguing fact that the hotel is situated on the site of Gemini Film Studios, which have produced films here since the 1940's.

Der Pool auf dem Dach des Park Chennai ist mehr als nur ein Schwimmbad. Die Betreiber des Hotels haben hier einen ungewöhnlichen Ort geschaffen, an dem die Gäste nicht nur baden können, sondern an dem auch kulinarische Veranstaltungen stattfinden. Das Becken und das direkt daneben liegende Restaurant „Aqua" verbinden sich zu einer multifunktionalen Einheit. Bei einer Barbecue-Party etwa kann der Blick über die Stadt schweifen. Große Tagesbetten laden zum bequemen Herumlümmeln ein und bieten Schutz vor der Sonne und – wenn man die seitlichen Vorhänge zuzieht – vor neugierigen Blicken anderer Gäste. Zu der besonderen Atmosphäre trägt vielleicht auch die Tatsache bei, dass das Hotel auf dem ehemaligen Gelände der Gemini-Filmstudios liegt, die seit den 40er-Jahren hier drehten.

the fullerton | singapore

DESIGN: Keys & Dowdeswell, Architects 61 Hisher Bedner Associates

The Fullerton Hotel inhabits a building from 1928; presenting itself as a luxury contemporary hotel, it refreshes its guests with its simplicity, peace and tranquility, combining both design and comfort together. It is located in the center of the financial district, making a contrast between movement and settlement; the massive Doric columns accentuate the settlement and the rooftop pool clearly frames the movement. The city's skyline and river promenade become another level in this hotel. It is the luxury of view that defines The Fullerton as a whole, overlooking the newest skyscrapers and historical bridges. It is as if one could swim throughout time.

Das Hotel befindet sich in einem Gebäude aus dem Jahre 1928. Mit Schlichtheit, Komfort, Eleganz und zeitgenössischem Design präsentiert sich das Fullerton als ein Luxushotel, das seine Gäste mit Frieden und Ruhe umgibt und verwöhnt. Es liegt im Herzen des Bankenviertels und setzt einen Ruhepunkt inmitten der Hektik, ein Eindruck, der von den schweren dorischen Säulen unterstützt wird. Vom Rooftop-Pool aus kann man das Treiben der Stadt, etwa an der Uferpromenade, beobachten und über die Skyline blicken. Man sieht sowohl die neuesten Wolkenkratzer als auch historische Brücken; es ist, als könne man durch die Zeiten schwimmen.

mandarin oriental munich | munich . germany

DESIGN: Helmut Jahn

Make the most of this city centre, roof top pool while the sun shines bright in the high sky as it understandably closes for the deep, central European winters. Appreciate the unique nature of the location; overlooking the steeply pitched, red tiled roofs and cobbled streets of the Altstadt. The soaring plane trees in the biergarten of the city's famous Hofbräuhaus and the luxury brands for sale on nearby Maximilianstrasse could also be seen from here. One step away is the twin towers of the Frauenkirche and the swath of green that is the Englischer Garten alongside the River Isar. And away to the South, the peaks of the Alps glisten invitingly. The use of the blue & white Bavarian colors in the both the pool tiles and the poolside furniture is used here. The oblong pool can be reached from the stainless steel steps from the sun terrace. The pool has a wide infinity edge, with a long boundary, where a glass wall affords security. The elegant white chairs and loungers are intermingled with planters of lavender and topiary worked box plants. Guests lingering to admire the view are able to order drinks from the tented bar or join the weekly caipirinha evenings.

Exklusiver könnte ein Schwimmbad in der bayerischen Metropole kaum platziert sein. Vom Dach des Hotels überblickt man die spitzgiebeligen roten Ziegeldächer und die gepflasterten Straßen der Münchner Altstadt, die hoch aufragenden Platanen im Biergarten des berühmten Hofbräuhauses und die Luxusgeschäfte in der nahen Maximilianstraße. Nur einen Steinwurf entfernt finden sich die beiden Türme der Frauenkirche und der Englische Garten. Und weiter südlich glitzern einladend die Alpengipfel. Die Verwendung der Landesfarben Blau und Weiß bei den Pool-Fliesen und den Möbeln am Beckenrand ist kein Zufall. Den Pool – ein kompaktes, funktionales und erhöhtes Rechteck – erreicht man von der Sonnenterrasse aus über Stahlstufen. Er scheint keinen Rand zu besitzen und eine Längsseite schließt mit der Dachkante ab, wo eine Glaswand die nötige Sicherheit bietet. Zwischen den eleganten weißen Stühlen und Liegen befinden sich Pflanztöpfe mit Lavendel und Buchsbäumen. Gäste, die von hier den Ausblick genießen, können sich aus der Zeltbar Drinks bestellen oder an den wöchentlich stattfindenden Caipirinha-Abenden teilnehmen.

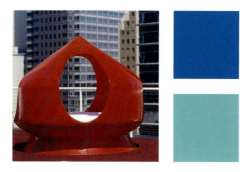

the standard downtown | los angeles . usa
DESIGN: Koning-Eizenberg Architecture

This hotel inhabits the elegant former headquarters of the Superior Oil Company from the 1950's. It is downtown L.A.'s intimate public space. The architectural designed was based on advertising, movies and fashion from the '50's and '60's, combined with modern minimal design; it integrates individuals from a standard perception into a contemporary mood, where the city's energy vibrates on the water-beds on the rooftop of this building, carved out of the marble clad mechanical existing penthouse. It now functions as the ultimate roof-top pool and lounge party, where the vision goes beyond into the adjacent building's wall where the screening epic of "Wizard of Oz" is projected and out into the high-rise towers that surround this space bringing both into reality.

Dieses Hotel befindet sich in der eleganten ehemaligen Hauptniederlassung der Superior Oil Company aus den 50er-Jahren. Es ist ein heimeliger, öffentlicher Ort im Zentrum von Los Angeles. Die Architektur ist von der Werbung, den Filmen und der Mode aus den 50er- und 60er-Jahren inspiriert – kombiniert mit modernem, minimalistischem Design; die Menschen werden aus ihrer herkömmlichen Wahrnehmung in eine zeitgenössische versetzt: Die vibrierende Energie der Stadt ist etwa auf den Wasserbetten auf der Dachterrasse zu spüren, die aus dem bestehenden, mit Marmor verkleideten Penthouse entstanden sind. Jetzt findet man dort den Rooftop-Pool mit Lounge Party, von wo aus der Blick zur angrenzenden Gebäudewand wandert, auf die das Epos „Der Zauberer von Oz" projiziert wird – und zu den umgebenden Hochhäusern, die einen in die Realität zurückholen.

habita | mexico city . mexico

DESIGN: Enrique Norten, Bernardo Gómez-Pimienta, TEN Arquitectos

You are in the heart of one of the world's largest metropolises, Mexico City; more precisely, the fashionable Polanco district – think luxury brands and media agencies – Mexico's answer to Fifth Avenue or Bond Street. Your pool is your getaway; your sanctuary from the draining retail experience and teeming urban masses below. Neither lap nor plunge, you are invited to just lounge beside this elegant white pool and gaze out at the distant skyscrapers. Or take the time to absorb the full benefit of your shiatsu or tuina treatment at the adjacent Aqua Spa. Do nothing. Splash the water to watch the sparkling striations of bright sunlight mimic the black and white organic pattern of the ceramic end-panels by Dutch artist Jan Hendrix. Float lazily alongside the opaque glass wall of the pool that makes up the sheer exterior of the building. Wander up the spiral staircase to the overlooking Area Bar, an extension of the pool deck below with the same wide hardwood boards. Here white sofas and armchairs take the place of the sun loungers. Sip a cocktail with the stylish crowd or, on cooler nights, curl up beside the open fire – a stunning and slash of open flame in a white block.

Das vornehme Polanco-Viertel ist Mexikos Antwort auf die Fifth Avenue oder Bond Street. Weder New York noch London haben jedoch ein Habita. Ein mit einer milchigen Glasfassade umhülltes Designhotel, dessen Hauptattraktion die offene Lounge mit Pool auf dem Dach ist. Er ist zu klein für Kopfsprünge und auch ungeeignet für sportliches Schwimmen. Aber das ist auch nicht der eigentliche Zweck. Vielmehr geht es um Entspannung in der Großstadt, einfach nur am Rand dieses eleganten, weißen Pools herumliegen und die Wolkenkratzer in der Ferne betrachten. Oder sich bei einer Tuina-Behandlung im angrenzenden Aqua Spa verwöhnen lassen. Mit den Füßen im Wasser plantschen und beobachten, wie die funkelnden Sonnenstrahlen das schwarzweiße Muster der Keramikplatten imitieren, die der niederländische Künstler Jan Hendrix entworfen hat. Über eine Wendeltreppe gelangt man zur darüber liegenden Area-Bar – eine Verlängerung der Pool-Ebene aus den gleichen breiten Hartholzplanken. Hier ersetzen weiße Sofas und Sessel die Sonnenliegen, und wenn die Nächte kühler sind, lodert das Feuer im offenen Kamin in einem weißen Block.

es hotel | rome . italy
DESIGN: King Roselli Architetti

It is located in the city centre near Termini Station; Es Hotel is a combination of an urban landscape, style, design & technology. This hotel - rare in the world - has an archeological site, immediately responds to its context by respecting the site and suspending itself above the street level, claiming its individuality. The pool in this hotel directs one into the urban streetscape of Rome bringing both city lights and the light effects from the façade out into the pool, reflecting to form this individual space.

Diese Unterkunft liegt im Stadtzentrum in der Nähe des Bahnhofs Termini; das es.hotel ist eine Kombination aus urbaner Landschaft, Stil, Design und Technik. Dieses Hotel besitzt – was weltweit nur sehr selten vorkommt – eine archäologische Fundstelle und reagiert darauf, indem es seine Umgebung respektiert und sich davon abhebt; es unterstreicht seine Individualität über das Straßenniveau hinaus. Der Hotelpool versetzt einen in die urbane Straßenlandschaft von Rom, in seinem Wasser spiegeln sich sowohl die Straßenbeleuchtung als auch die Lichteffekte von der Fassade, sodass ein einmaliger Ort entsteht.

natural curves

ikal del mar | playa xcalacoco . mexico
DESIGN: Ramiro Altorre

Ikal del Mar is an exclusive place where the ocean's waves blend-in with the inner individual's spirit. This secluded seaside resort was carved out from the primitive Mayan jungle, preserving its powerful natural site and beliefs; this nested space consists of twenty-nine private luxury villas each with a private plunge-pool and is constructed with natural wood and indigenous stones from the area. The natural sound waves of the ocean reflect themselves out into a curvilinear public pool with a direct connection to a white-sand beach. This tranquil ambiance provokes the inner peace and energy to weave outside from the world into the perfect background of the Caribbean Sea across one's soul.

Ikal del Mar ist ein exklusiver Ort, an dem die Wellen des Ozeans eine meditative Stimmung verbreiten. Dieses abgeschiedene Küstenresort wurde behutsam aus dem Dschungel herausgeschnitten, mit möglichst geringem Eingriff in die Natur. Die in sich abgeschlossene Anlage besteht aus 29 privaten Luxusvillen, jede mit eigenem Pool. Sie wurden aus Holz und Stein, der in der Umgebung vorkommt, erbaut. Am geschwungenen öffentlichen Pool mit direkter Verbindung zum weißen Sandstrand ist der Klang von Ozeanwellen zu hören. Das friedvolle Ambiente bringt innere Ruhe und Energie, um abseits der Welt in die perfekte Landschaft der Karibik einzutauchen.

katikies | santorin . greece

DESIGN: Ilias Apostolidis, Giorgos Lizardos, Nikos Tzelepis

Santorini is perhaps the best known of Greece's Cycladic Islands and steeped in myths. It was here that the civilization sunk into the sea, possibly giving rise to the story of the lost city of Atlantis. Today the name Santorini stands for romantic associations all on its own. The Hotel Katikies provides experiences that live up to the reputation of peace and sensuality associated with the story of Atlantis. As twilight envelopes the surrounding seas, the air cools, and pools and warm effervescent water become illuminated in bright green. A private individual masseuse, clad in white, approaches to knead and invigorate tired muscles with precious oils. By the poolside, massages are offered as part of the hotel's service. One of Katikies most distinguishing features is the terraced design, with rooms, pools and niches on many levels. It is like a tiny whitewashed village set on a cliff, with winding stairs and passageways everywhere. Dazzling blue waters lap the rocks 100 meters below with dramatic sunsets.

Das mythenumrankte Santorini ist die wahrscheinlich bekannteste griechische Kykladeninsel. Hier soll die Zivilisation in den Tiefen des Meeres verschwunden sein und hier wurde wahrscheinlich die Geschichte um das versunkene Atlantis geboren. Heute wird der Name Santorini mit Romantik in Verbindung gebracht. Wenn die Dämmerung das umgebende Meer einhüllt, wird die Luft kühler und das warme, sprudelnde Wasser der Pools wird hellgrün erleuchtet. Am Poolrand werden Massagen als Bestandteil des Hotelservice angeboten. Eine weiß gekloidetc Privatmasseurin knetet müde Muskeln und belebt sie mit wertvollen Ölen. Eines der herausragendsten Merkmale von Katikies ist seine terrassenförmige Anlage: Zimmer, Pools und Nischen liegen auf vielen Ebenen. Es wirkt wie ein kleines weißes Dorf auf einer Klippe – mit gewundenen Treppen und Durchgängen überall. Während eines spektakulären Sonnenuntergangs schlagen 100 Meter weiter unten kristallblaue Wellen gegen die Felsen.

the raleigh | miami . usa
DESIGN: Lawrence Murray

The flashback into the 40's still perfectly fits the Raleigh, the first white skyscraper hotel in Miami. André Balasz and the creative team of Hotels AB brought the Raleigh back to radiance, contributing to the new revival of Miami Beach. The pool must be given a key role here. Provided with new black paint, the double rim of the pool emphasizes its sexy form. The area around the pool was demarcated and colorfully freshened with a multitude of lush palm trees. The candy-colored accents of the orange chairs in the pool café, blue porthole windows and even just the playfully useless, red lifesavers on the brilliant white pool pavilion have the same effect. Blue-white and beige-white striped reclining chairs and similar sunshades set even more of these unobtrusive classical accents. The light of Chinese lanterns complement the evenings out in this new revival.

Der Flashback in die 40er-Jahre steht dem Raleigh, dem ersten weißen Wolkenkratzerhotel von Miami Beach, noch immer wunderbar. André Balasz und ein Kreativteam von „Hotels AB" brachten es vor kurzem wieder zum Strahlen, sodass das Raleigh seinen unübersehbaren Beitrag zum Revival von Miami Beach leisten wird. Eine Schlüsselrolle kommt dabei sicher dem Pool zu. Lawrence Murray Dixon muss die Kurven von Pin-up-Girls vor Augen gehabt haben, als er diese Badelandschaft entwarf. Mit neuem schwarzen Lack versehen, umschmeichelt und betont der doppelte Rand des Beckens dessen sexy Form. Die Umgebung des Pools wurde mit vielen üppigen Palmen blickdicht abgegrenzt und farblich aufgefrischt. Den gleichen Effekt haben die orangefarbenen Stühle am Pool-Café, blaue Bullaugenfenster oder auch nur die neckisch unnützen, roten Rettungsreifen am strahlend weißen Pool-Pavillon. Blauweiß und beigeweiß gestreifte Liegestühle und ebensolche Sonnenschirme setzen noch mehr von diesen unaufdringlichen klassischen Akzenten. Abends spenden Lampions weiches Licht.

north island | north island . seychelles

DESIGN: Silvio Rech & Lesley Cartens Architecture

A hotel, an island – only two words are required to describe the concept of North Island. The proprietors of the resort, a group including the German, Wolfgang Burre, owns the entire island, and they take advantage of this unique opportunity to preserve the endemic flora and fauna. For this reason, they permitted themselves the luxury of building only eleven guest villas on the entire island. The buildings, constructed using traditional forms and natural materials, harmonize so well with the surrounding landscape that they are barely detectable from even a short distance. Located on the crest of a small rise is the main pool. Its curved form seems to be a continuation of the contours of the hilly terrain. On the upper slope, the pool is enclosed by a wooden deck where comfortable lounge chairs are available. The lower slope is enclosed by a granite wall over which water quietly ripples. From this seemingly edgeless brink of the pool, guests can look over the palm tree crowns while swimming and marvel at the view over the vast ocean. With its length of 45 meters, the pool is perfectly suitable for a good swim workout. Who needs the exquisite white beach located just a few steps down the slope?

Ein Hotel, eine Insel – so lässt sich mit nur zwei Worten das Konzept von North Island beschreiben. Den Eignern des Resorts, einer Gruppe um den Deutschen Wolfgang Burre, gehört die gesamte Insel und sie nutzen diese Chance, um ihre Ursprünglichkeit mit allen Tier- und Pflanzenarten zu erhalten. Deshalb leisteten sie sich auch den Luxus, auf der ganzen Insel nur 11 Gästevillen zu errichten. Die Gebäude passen mit ihren traditionellen Formen und natürlichen Materialien so gut in die Landschaft, dass sie schon aus geringer Entfernung kaum mehr zu erkennen sind. An einer leicht erhöhten Stelle liegt der Hauptpool. Mit seiner geschwungenen Form scheint er die Höhenlinien des hügeligen Geländes nachzuzeichnen. An der Hangoberseite wird er von einem Holzdeck eingefasst, auf dem komfortable Liegestühle bereitstehen, an der Hangunterseite hingegen von einer Mauer aus Granitsteinen, über die das Wasser leise nach unten plätschert. Über diesen scheinbar randlosen Abschluss des Beckens hinweg kann der Gast beim Baden durch Palmenkronen hindurch aufs offene Meer schauen. Mit 45 Metern eignet sich der Pool durchaus, um in sportlichen Zügen lange Bahnen zu schwimmen. Wer braucht da noch den traumhaft weißen Sandstrand, der nur ein paar Schritte hangabwärts liegt?

shompole | amboseli . kenya

D E S I G N :   Anthony Russell, Neil Rocher, Elizabeth Warner

The name of the resort already indicates its location: "Shompole" means "brown land", and the accommodations are located in the middle of the desert on the boundary between Kenya and Tanzania. Here, tourists not accustomed to the hot climate find protection from the sun under the tall straw roofs, which also partially cover the outdoor pools. Guests can cool off in the water without being exposed to the searing sun. Gently curved pools are nestled between dry and barren tree trunks that are randomly placed and bear the roofs. The design of the facility is altogether quite unusual. Its founder, Anthony Russel, manages the resort together with the local African people, the Massai, who incorporated their traditional forms and craftsmanship when building the accommodations. The houses resemble old straw huts and nomadic tent constructions. They are open so the guest feels the cooling wind while relaxing in the shade and enjoying the view of the surrounding desert wilderness.

Der Name des Resorts gibt bereits einen Hinweis auf seinen Standort: „Shompole" bedeutet „braunes Land", denn die Unterkünfte liegen mitten in der Wüste – an der Grenze zwischen Kenia und Tansania. Touristen, die das heiße Klima nicht gewohnt sind, finden unter den hohen Strohdächern Schutz, die sogar teilweise die Wasserbecken im Freien überspannen. So können die Gäste zur Abkühlung ein Bad nehmen, ohne dabei der Sonne ausgesetzt zu sein. Die weich geschwungenen Pools schmiegen sich zwischen dürre Baumstämme, die – in freier Anordnung verteilt – als Pfosten der Dächer dienen. Überhaupt ist die Gestaltung der Anlage sehr ungewöhnlich. Ihr Gründer Anthony Russell betreibt sie gemeinsam mit den Bewohnern der Region, den Massai, die auch bei der Errichtung der Unterkünfte ihre traditionellen Formen und Handwerkstechniken einbrachten. Die Häuser ähneln alten Strohhütten, teilweise erinnern sie auch an nomadische Zeltbauten. Sie sind sehr offen, sodass man im Schatten sitzend sowohl den kühlenden Wind spüren als auch den Blick in die umgebende wilde Natur genießen kann.

four seasons resort punta mita | punta mita . mexico
DESIGN: Diego Villasenor, Wimberly Allison Tong

The Four Seasons Punta Mita is built in the midst of a 400 hectare areal in the Mexican ‚casitas' style. The facilities main attraction is an 18-hole golf course designed by Jack Nicklaus adjoining the virtually unending, gleaming white sandy beach on the Pacific coast. The inner-life of the rooms and suites was designed by the interior decorator Maria Isabel Gómez from Guadalajara in the style of Mexican residencies. Especially the suites impress through their spacious room layout, own terraces and private pools. The hotel's large, sweeping Infinity-Pool spreads out below the main building. With a constant water temperature of 30°C, this bathing-scape is a cozy alternative to the generally chillier Pacific. A whirlpool, integrated into the pool scenery, and a Kneipp pool are offered here as an embarkation into the Punta Mita spa wellness-program. During siesta on the chaise lounges in the penumbra of the palapas with a view of the horizon over the pool, the waiters attend with personal towels and even cooling facial sprays. At best, the ambience might possibly be rarefied by a snack at the Ketsi pool bar under the shady palm roof.

Das Four Seasons Punta Mita ist im Stil mexikanischer „Casitas" inmitten eines 400 Hektar großen Areals gebaut. Das Aushängeschild der Anlage ist der von Jack Nicklaus entworfene 18-Loch-Golfplatz, der an den schier endlosen, leuchtend weißen Sandstrand an der Pazifikküste anschließt. Das Innenleben der Zimmer und Suiten gestaltete die Innenarchitektin Maria Isabel Gómez aus Guadalajara im Stil mexikanischer Residenzen. Vor allem die Suiten überzeugen durch großzügige Raumeinteilung, eigene Terrassen und zum Teil private Pools. Unterhalb des Hauptgebäudes breitet sich der große geschwungene Infinity-Pool des Hotels aus. Mit einer Wassertemperatur von konstant 30 °C ist diese Badelandschaft eine wohlige Alternative zum meist deutlich frischeren Pazifik. Ein Whirlpool, in die Poollandschaft integriert, und ein Kneippbecken bieten sich hier als Einstieg in das Wellnessprogramm im Spa von Punta Mita. Zur Siesta auf einer der Chaiselongues im Halbschatten der Palapas mit Blick über den Pool zum Horizont reicht einem das Personal Handtücher und kühlende Gesichtssprays. Das Ambiente lässt sich allenfalls durch einen Snack an der Pool-Bar „Ketsi" unter dem schattigen Palmendach verfeinern.

las ventanas al paraiso | los cabos . mexico
DESIGN: Wilson & Associates

Those who enter this hotel are tempted to not leave the grounds during their entire stay. The hotel offers not only access to a sandy beach, tennis and golf, snorkeling and fishing, but also individual yoga classes and aroma massages performed outside. The 61 suites complete with fireplaces, marble showers and whirlpools create a relaxing atmosphere. Beach suite patios, shielded from view, entice guests to a dip in their private whirlpool during the day and to observe the depths of the universe through a telescope at night. For those not content with splashing around in the water, preferring instead to swim a few laps, the central resort pool is the place to go. More a pool landscape, the pool stretches like a natural lake, curving around several peninsulas on which either cacti grow or lounge chairs await their guests. Swimming laps – or rather curves – around this lake while looking out over the water, which, due to Infinity-Edge, appears to blend into the ocean, is one of the greatest pleasures the hotel has to offer. The highlight, however, is to be seated on a submerged bar stool and enjoy a refreshing Margarita.

Wer dieses Hotel betritt, ist versucht, es während des ganzen Aufenthalts nicht mehr zu verlassen. Es bietet nicht nur Zugang zum Sandstrand, Tennis- und Golf-, Schnorchel- und Angelmöglichkeiten, sondern auch individuelle Yogakurse und Aromamassagen unter freiem Himmel. In den 61 Suiten schaffen Kaminfeuer, Marmorduschen und Whirlpool eine entspannte Atmosphäre. Nicht einsehbare Terrassen in den Strandsuiten laden tagsüber zu einer Abkühlung im privaten Whirlpool ein, während sich nachts mit einem Teleskop der Sternenhimmel beobachten lässt. Wer jedoch nicht nur im Wasser plantschen, sondern ein paar Meter schwimmen möchte, sollte den zentralen Pool des Resorts aufsuchen. Eigentlich ist es eher schon eine Pool-Landschaft, denn das Becken windet sich wie ein natürlicher See in weitem Schwung um mehrere Halbinseln, auf denen Kakteen wachsen oder aber einfach die Liegestühle stehen. Hier seine Bahnen – pardon Kurven – zu schwimmen und dabei über die Wasserfläche zu blicken, die dank Infinity-Edge fließend ins Meer überzugehen scheint, gehört zu den großen Vergnügen, die das Hotel bietet. Die Krönung aber ist, auf einem Unterwasserhocker am Beckenrand Platz zu nehmen und einen Margarita zu trinken.

architects & designers, hotels, photo credits

cover front   Martin Nicholas Kunz
cover back courtesy GHM Hotels & Resorts
table of content   Thomas Hausberg (map)
introduction   courtesy Wave Design,
                                 Singapore (1)
                       Martin Nicholas Kunz (2)
                      courtesy P & O Resorts (3)
                          courtesy Life Gallery (4)

imprint

Bibliographic information published by Die Deutsche Bibliothek
Die Deutsche Bibliothek lists this publication in the Deutsche
Nationalbibliografie; detailed bibliographic data are available in
the Internet at http://dnb.ddb.de

ISBN 3-89986-038-1

Printed in Austria

Editorial Direction | Martin Nicholas Kunz
Editorial Coordination & Research | Ursula Dietmair,
Patricia Massó
Copy editing: Martina Fiess (deutsch), Ade Team (english)
Texts (pages) | Michelle Galindo (Introduction, 112, 128, 134,
140, 144, 148); Ursula Dietmair (16, 18, 20, 26, 32, 70,
82, 114, 122, 150, 160); Guy Dittrich (40, 46, 74, 86, 96,
100, 116, 132, 136); Christian Schönwetter (8, 12, 14, 36,
50, 54, 60, 64, 66, 78, 90, 104, 106, 108, 110, 124, 152,
156, 162)
Translations | Ade Team, Stuttgart
Layout | Michelle Galindo
Production & Imaging | Jan Hausberg, Käthe Nennstiel,
Susanne Olbrich
Printing | Vorarlberger Verlagsanstalt AG, Dornbirn Austria

avedition GmbH
Königsallee 57 | 71638 Ludwigsburg | Germany
p +49-7141-1477391 | f +49-7141-1477399
http://www.avedition.de | info@avedition.de

Further information and links at www.bestdesigned.com

Special thanks to

Lina Lee Banyan Tree Seychelles | Christina von Berg,
Vigilius Mountain Resort | Gian Luca   Bertilaccio,
Casa del Mar | Wolfgang Burre, North Island | Gordon Campbell-
Gray | Jennifer Chaing, The Lalu | Julia Coral, Mandarin
Oriental Munich | Elizabeth Crompton-Batt, Cowley Manor |
Scott M. Crouch | Trina Dingler-Ebert, Amanresorts | Andre
Diogo, Estalagem da Ponta do Sol | Asli Eke, Hillside Su |
Pauline Engelse, Crowne Plaza Resort Funchal | Stephanie
Fendler, Hyatt Hotels & Resorts | Bruno Franchi, Matteo Thun
Studio | Philippe Frutiger, Lenkerhof Alpine Resort | V V Giri,
The Park Chennai | Neeta Guptar, Devi Garh | Katja Hekkala,
Choupana Hills | Putru Indrawati, Four Seasons Resorts Bali |
Claudia Knapp, Therme Vals | Nina Kumana, Amanresorts |
Fiona Lane, Banyan Tree Seychelles | Heinz Legler, Verana |
Veronique Lièvre, Verana | Rennie Loh, The Fullerton Singapore
| Michael Di Lonardo, Vigilius Mountain Resort | Hansjörg Maier,
The Legian & The Club at The Legian | Christoph Mares,
Mandarin Oriental Munich | Moisés Micha, Deseo & Habita |
Philippe Moreau, Choupana Hills | David Murray, North Island
| Larry van Ooyen, The Lalu | Chania Paterson, Shompole
| Ignacio Pérez, Maricel | Poddar Family | Abigail Rivera,
Ikal del Mar | Howard Rombough, One Aldwych | Arianna
Roscioli, Es Hotel | Sanctuary Resorts | Anke Schaffelhuber,
North Island | Romana Schmidt, Chedi Muscat | Schubert
& Schubert, Hamburg | Karina Shima, Park Hyatt Tokyo |
Frederic F. Simon, Alila Ubud | Deepanita Singh, Grand Hyatt
Mumbai | German del Sol | Simone De Soledad, Design Suites
| Angelos Sotiropoulos, Life Gallery | Mira Szarata, design
hotels Bali | Eren Talu, Hillside Su | Matteo Thun | Rainata Tjoa,
The Balé | Murat Tufan, Hillside Su | Eleni Tzanou, Katikies |
Neslihan Ugurlu, Hillside Su | Ferdinand Wortelboer, Amanjena
| ZFL Team, London & Munich | Peter Zumthor | Annaliesa
Zumthor, Therme Vals

Martin Nicholas Kunz

1957 born in Hollywood.
Founder of fusion publishing
creating content for architecture, design, travel and
lifestyle publications.

best designed hotels:
Asia Pacific
Americas
Europe I (urban)
Europe II (countryside)

best designed
wellness hotels:
Asia Pacific
Americas
Europe
Africa & Middle East

All books are released in
German and English